Louise Imogen Guiney

A Little English Gallery

Louise Imogen Guiney

A Little English Gallery

ISBN/EAN: 9783744651714

Printed in Europe, USA, Canada, Australia, Japan

Cover: Foto ©Thomas Meinert / pixelio.de

More available books at **www.hansebooks.com**

A LITTLE ENGLISH GALLERY

BY
LOUISE IMOGEN GUINEY

NEW YORK
HARPER AND BROTHERS
MDCCCXCIV

TO
EDMUND GOSSE
THIS FRIENDLY TRESPASS ON HIS FIELDS

PREFATORY NOTE

THE studies in this book are chosen from a number written at irregular intervals, and from sheer interest in their subjects, long ago. Portions of them, or rough drafts of what has since been wholly remodelled from fresher and fuller material at first hand, have appeared within five years in *The Atlantic Monthly*, *Macmillan's*, *The Catholic World*, and *Poet-Lore;* and thanks are due the magazines for permission to reprint them. Yet more cordial thanks, for kind assistance on biographical points, belong to the Earl of Powis; the Rev. R. H. Davies, Vicar of old St. Luke's, Chelsea; the Rev. T. Vere Bayne, of Christchurch, and H. E. D. Blakiston, Esq., of Trinity College, Oxford; T. W. Lyster, Esq., of the National Library of Ireland; Aubrey de Vere Beauclerk, Esq.; Miss Langton, of Langton-by-Spilsby; the Vicars of Dauntsey, Enfield Highway, and Montgomery, and especially those of High Ercall and Speke; and the many others in England through whose courtesy and patience the tracer of these unimportant sketches has been able to make them approximately life-like.

1894

CONTENTS

CHAP.		PAGE
I.	LADY DANVERS (1561–1627) . . .	1
II.	HENRY VAUGHAN (1621–1695) . . .	53
III.	GEORGE FARQUHAR (1677–1707) . .	119
IV.	TOPHAM BEAUCLERK (1739–1780) AND BENNET LANGTON (1741–1800) . .	171
V.	WILLIAM HAZLITT (1778–1830) . .	229

I
LADY DANVERS
1561–1627

LADY DANVERS

R. MATTHEW ARNOLD somewhere devotes a grateful sentence to the women who have left a fragrance in literary history, and whose loss of long ago can yet inspire men of to-day with indescribable regret. Lady Danvers is surely one of these. As John Donne's dear friend, and George Herbert's mother, she has a double poetic claim, like her unforgotten contemporary, Mary Sidney, for whom was made an everlasting epitaph. If Dr. Donne's fraternal fame have not quite the old lustre of the incomparable Sir Philip's, it is, at least, a greater honor to own Herbert for son than to have perpetuated the race of Pembroke. Nor is it an inharmonious thing to remember, in thus calling up, in order to rival it, the sweet

memory of "Sidney's sister," that Herbert and Pembroke have long been, and are yet, married names.

Magdalen, the youngest child of Sir Richard Newport, and of Margaret Bromley, his wife, herself daughter of that Bromley who was Privy-Councillor, Lord Chief-Justice, and executor to Henry VIII., was born in High Ercall, Salop; the loss or destruction of parish registers leaves us but 1561-62 as the probable date. Of princely stock, with three sisters and an only brother, and heir to virtue and affluence, she could look with the right pride of unfallen blood upon "the many fair coats the Newports bear" over their graves at Wroxeter. It was the day of learned and thoughtful girls; and this girl seems to have been at home with book and pen, with lute and viol. She married, in the flower of her youth, Richard Herbert, Esquire, of Blache Hall, Montgomery, black-haired and black-bearded, as were all his line; a man of some intellectual training, and of noted courage, descended from a distinguished brother of the yet more distinguished Sir

Richard Herbert of Edward IV.'s time, and from the most ancient rank of Wales and England. At Eyton in Salop, in 1581, was born their eldest child, Edward, afterwards Lord Herbert of Cherbury, a writer who is still the puzzle and delight of Continental critics. He is said to have been a beautiful boy, and not very robust; his first speculation with his infant tongue was the piercing query: "How came I into this world?" But his next brother, Richard, was of another stamp; and went his frank, flashing, fighting way through Europe, "with scars of four-and-twenty wounds upon him, to his grave" at Bergen-op-Zoom, with William, the third son, following in his soldierly footsteps. Charles grew up reserved and studious, and died, like his paternal uncle, a dutiful Fellow of New College, Oxford. The fifth of these Herberts, "a soul composed of harmonies," as Cotton said of him, and destined to make the name beloved among all readers of English, was George, the poet, the saintly "parson of Fuggleston and Bemerton." Henry, his junior, with whom George had a sympathy peculiarly warm and long, became in his manhood Master of the Revels, and held the office for over fifty years. "You and I are alone left to brother it," Lord Herbert of Cherbury once wrote him, in a mood more tender than his wont, when all else of that radiant family had gone into dust. The youngest of Magdalen Newport's sons was Thomas, "a posthumous," traveller, sailor, and master of a ship in the war against Algiers. Elizabeth, Margaret, and Frances were the daughters, of whom Izaak Walton says, with satisfaction, that they lived to be examples of virtue, and to do good to their generation. None of them made an illustrious match. Margaret married a Vaughan. Frances secured unto herself the patronymic Brown, and was happily seconded by Elizabeth, George Herbert's "dear sick sister," who became Mistress Jones. In the south chancel transept of Montgomery Church, where Richard Herbert the elder had been buried three years before, there was erected in 1600, at his wife's cost, a large canopied alabaster altar-tomb, with two portrait-figures recumbent. All around it, in the quaint and affectionate boast of the age, are the small images of these seven sons and three daughters; "Job's number and Job's distribution," as she once remarked, and as her biographers failed not to repeat after her. But their kindred ashes are widely sundered, and "as content with six foot as with the moles of Adrianus." This at Montgomery is the only known representation of the Lady Magdalen. Her effigy lies at her husband's left, the palms folded, the eyes open, the full hair rolled back from a low brow, beneath a charming and simple head-dress. Nothing can be nobler than the whole look of the face, like her in her prime, and reminding one of her son's loving epithet, "my Juno." The short-sighted inscription upon the slab yet includes her name.

Never had an army of brilliant and requiring children a more excellent mother. "*Severa parens,*" her gentle George called her in his scholarly verses; and such she was, with the mingled sagacity and joyousness which made up her character. If we are to believe their own testimony, the leading members of her young family were of excessively peppery Cymric temperaments, and worthy to call out that "manlier part" of her which Dr. Donne, who had every opportunity of observing it in play, was so quick to praise. There is a passage in a letter of Sir Thomas Lacy, addressed to Edward Herbert, touching upon "the knowledge I had how ill you can digest the least indignity." "Holy George Herbert" himself, in 1618, commended to his dear brother Henry the gospel of self-honoring: "It is the part of a poor spirit to undervalue himself and blush." And physical courage went hand in hand with this blameless haughtiness of the Herberts, a pretty collateral proof of which may be adduced from a message of Sir Henry Jones to his brother-in-law, the other Henry just mentioned, concerning a gift for his little nephew. "If my cozen, William Herbert your sonne... be ready for the rideing of a horse, I will provide him with a Welch nagg that shall be as mettlesome as himself." There is no doubt that all this racial fire was fostered by one woman.

"Thou my root, and my most firm rock, O my mother!" George cried, long after in the *Parentalia*, aware that he owed to her his high ideals, and the strength of character which is born of self-discipline.

"God gave her," says one of her two devoted annalists, who we wish were not so brief and meagre of detail—"God gave her such a comeliness as though she was not proud of it, yet she was so content with it as not to go about to mend it by any art." Her fortune was large, her benevolence wide-spreading. All the countryside knew her for the living representative of the ever-hospitable houses of Newport and Bromley. "She gave not on some great days," continues Dr. Donne, "or at solemn goings abroad; but as God's true almoners, the sun and moon, that pass on in a continual doing of good; as she received her daily bread from God, so daily she distributed it, and imparted it to others." In these years of her wifehood and widowhood at Montgomery Castle (the "romancy place" dating from the eleventh century, and ruined, like the fine old house at High Ercall, during the

Civil Wars), and afterwards at Oxford and London, she reared her happy crew of boys and girls in an air of generosity and honor; training them to habits of hardiness and simplicity, and to the equal relish of work and play. "Herself with her whole family (as a church in that elect lady's house, to whom John wrote his second Epistle) did every Sabbath shut up the day at night with a general, with a cheerful singing of psalms." One may guess at young Richard's turmoil in-doors, and at the little Elizabeth's soft, patient ways, and think of George (on Sundays at any rate) as the child of content, "the contesseration of elegances" worthy Archdeacon Oley called him.

The fair and stately matron moving over them and among them was not without her prejudices. "I was once," Edward testifies, "in danger of drowning, learning to swim. My mother, upon her blessing, charged me never to learn swimming; telling me, further, that she had learned of more drowned than saved by it." Though the given reason failed to impress him, he adds, the commandment did; so that the accomplished Crichton of Cherbury, who understood alchemy, broke his way through metaphysics, and rode the Great Horse; the ambassador, author, and beau, to whom Ben Jonson sent his greeting:

> "What man art thou that art so many men,
> All-virtuous Herbert?"

even he lacked, on principle, the science of keeping himself alive in an alien element, because it had been pronounced less risky to die outright! It was a pretty paradox, and one which sets down our high-minded Magdalen as quite feminine, quite human.

Her Edward was matriculated in 1595 at University College, Oxford,* for which he seemed to retain no great partiality; he bequeathed his books, like a loyal Welshman, to Jesus College, instead, and

* Walton confuses this Edward Herbert with a namesake entered at Queen's College; and he follows the erring dates of the *Autobiography of Lord Herbert of Cherbury*. The boy's age is correctly given as fourteen in the college registers.

his manuscripts to the Bodleian Library. In 1598, when he was little more than seventeen, he was wedded to his cousin Mary Herbert, of St. Gillian in Monmouthshire. Her age was one-and-twenty; she was an heiress, enjoined by her father's will to marry a Herbert or forfeit her estates; she was also almost a philosopher. There was no wild affection on either side, but the marriage promised rather well, both persons having resources; and no real catastrophe befell either in after-life. Much as she desired the match for worldly motives, the chief promoter of it was too solicitous for her tall dreamer of a son, who underwent the pleasing peril of having Queen Bess clap him on the cheek, not to take the whole weight of conjugal direction on her own shoulders. Without undue officiousness, but with the masterly foresight of a shrewd saint, she moved to Oxford from Montgomery with her younger children and their tutors, in order to handle Mistress Herbert's husband during his minority. "She continued there with him," says Walton, in his *Life of George Herbert*, "and still kept him in a moderate awe of herself, and so much under her own eye as to see and converse with him daily; but she managed this power over him without any such rigid sourness as might make her company a torment to her child, but with such a sweetness and compliance with the recreations and pleasures of youth as did incline him willingly to spend much of his time in the company of his dear and careful mother."

It was during this stay that she contracted the chivalrous friendship which has embalmed her tranquil memory. Dr. John Donne (not ordained until 1614, and indeed not Dr. Donne then at all, but "Jack Donne," his profaner self) had been at Cadiz with Essex, and had wandered over the face of Europe; and he came back, accidentally, to Oxford during the most troubled year of his early prime. It was no strange place to him,* who had

---

* Donne had been in residence at both Universities, but took no degree at either, as he had scruples against accepting the conditions imposed. He was at that time, and until about 1593, like his parents, a Catholic. His

been, at eleven, the Pico della Mirandola of Hart Hall, and whose relatives seem to have resided always in the town. There and then, however, he cast his bright eye upon Excellence, and in his own phrase,

> " —dared love that, and say so, too,
> And forget the He and She."

We can do no better than cite a celebrated and beautiful passage, once more from Walton : " This amity, begun at this time and place, was not an amity that polluted their souls, but an amity made up of a chain of suitable inclinations and virtues; an amity like that of St. Chrysostom to his dear and virtuous Olympias, whom, in his letters, he calls his saint ; or an amity, indeed, more like that of St. Hierom to his Paula, whose affection to her was such that he turned poet in his old age, and then made her epitaph, wishing all his body were turned into tongues that he might declare her just praises to

father was of Welsh descent : a fact which may have borne its share in attracting him towards the Herberts.

posterity." How these words remind one of the sweet historic mention which Condivi gives to the relations between Vittoria Colonna and Michelangelo! The little English idyl of friendship and the great Italian one run parallel in much.

Donne's trenchant *Satires*, some of the earliest and very best in the language, were already written, and he was not without the hint of fame. Born in 1573, he was but eight years the senior of Edward Herbert, and not more than a dozen years the junior of Edward Herbert's mother. To her two sons, also, who were to figure as men of letters, he was sincerely attached from the first, and had a marked and lasting influence on their minds. Donne had the superabundance of mental power which Mr. Minto has pointed out as the paradoxical cause of his failure to become a great poet. He was a three-storied soul, as the French say: a spirit of many sides and moods, a life-long dreamer of good and bad dreams. To his restless, incisive intelligence his contemporaries, with Jonson and Carew at their head, bowed in hyperboles of acclaim.

He had a changeful conscience, often antagonized and often appeased. There was a strain in him of strong joy, for he was descended through his mother from pleasant John Heywood the dramatist, and from the father of that great and merry-hearted gentleman, Sir Thomas More. If ever man needed vitality to buoy him over sorrows heavy and vast, it was Donne in his "yeasting youth." Thrown, through no fault but his own, from his old footholds of religion and occupation, and unable, despite his versatile and alert genius, to grind a steady living from the hard mills of the world, he was in the midst of a bitter plight when the friends worthy of him found a heavenly opportunity which they did not let go by, and made his acceptance of their favor a rich gift unto themselves. Foremost among these, besides Lady Herbert, were Sir Robert Drury of Drury Lane, and a kinsman, Sir Francis Woolly, of Pirford, Surrey, fated to die in his youth, both of whom gave the Donnes, for some nine consecutive years, the use of their princely houses. John Donne had been in the service of the Chancellor, Lord Ellesmere, and lost place and purse by the opposition to his marriage with his "*lectissima dilectissimaque,*" Anne More, who was Lady Ellesmere's niece, the daughter of Sir George More of Loxly, Lieutenant of the Tower, and probably a distant cousin of his own. No reverses, however, could beat the pathetic cheer out of him. "Anne Donne,* undone," was one of his inveterate teary jests over the state of things at home. He wrote once, with sickness, poverty, and despair at his elbow: "If God should ease us with burials, I know not how to perform even that. But I flatter myself that I am dying, too, for I cannot waste faster than by such griefs." Five of his twelve children passed before their father to the grave, the good domestic daughter Constance upholding him always, and keeping the house together. But just as hope dawned with his appointment to the Lectureship of Lincoln's Inn, heavenward suddenly, with her youngest-born, in 1617, went his dear

* Anne Donne, it may be remarked, was also the name of Cowper's mother.

and faithful wife, whom he laid to rest in St. Clement Danes.

About the time when the remorseful old queen died disdainfully on her chamber-floor at Richmond, the necessities of this family called for daily succors, and with a simple and noble delicacy they were supplied. Nor did they cease. Magdalen Herbert was a " bountiful benefactor," Donne "as grateful an acknowledger." His first letter to her from Mitcham in Surrey, dated July 10, 1607, is made up of terse, tender thanks, in his heart's own odd language. He sends her an enclosure of sonnets and hymns, "lost to us," says Walton, movingly, "but doubtless they were such as they two now sing in heaven." Dr. Grosart, with a great show of justice, claims that the sequence called *La Corona*, and familiar to latter-day readers, are the identical sonnets passed from one to the other. During this same month of July we know that, paying a call in his "London, plaguey London," and finding his friend abroad,* Dr. Donne consoled

---

* Sir Richard Baker's *Chronicle*, 1684, mentions Dr.

himself by leaving a courtliest message:
"Your memory is a state-cloth and presence which I reverence, though you be away;" and went back after to his "sallads and onions" at Mitcham, or to his solitary lodgings near Whitehall.

The attachment, close and deferent on both sides, was continued without a breach, and with the intention, at least, of "almost daily letters." Thoreau, quoting Chaucer, so saluted Mrs. Emerson: "You have helped to keep my life on loft." No meaner service than this was his dear lady's to John Donne, often heretofore astray in the slough of doubt and dissipation; she fed more than his little children, clothed more than his body, and fostered anew in him that faith in humanity which is the well-spring of good works. He was not a poet of Leigh Hunt's innocent temperament, who could accept benefits gladly and gracefully from any appreciator; his soul dwelt too remote and proud in her accustomed citadels. But this loving help, thrust upon

Donne as one of his "heroic Grecians," and adds, in the same breath, that he was "a great visitor of ladies."

him, he took with dignity, and after 1621, when he was able, in his own person, to befriend others, he gave back gallantly to mankind the blessings he once received from two or three. It was something for Magdalen Herbert to have saved a master-name to English letters, and kept in his unique place the poet, interesting beyond many, whose fantastic but real force swayed generations of thinking and singing men; it was something, also, to have won in return the words which were his gold coin of payment. Nowhere is Donne's sentiment more genuine, his workmanship more happy and less complex, than in the verses dedicated to her blameless name. They have a lucidity unsurpassed among the yet straightforward lyrics of their day. Drayton's self, who died in the same year with Donne, might have addressed to the lady of Eyton so much of his noble extravagance;

> "Queens hereafter shall be glad to live
> Upon the alms of thy superfluous praise."

Yet in these eulogies, as in most of the graver contemporaneous poems of the sort, there is little personality to be detected; the homage has rather a floating outline, an unapproaching music, exquisite and awed. Donne gives, sometimes, the large Elizabethan measure:

"Is there any good which is not she?"

In the so-called *Elegy, The Autumnal*, written on leaving Oxford, he starts off with a well-known cherishable strophe:

"No spring nor summer beauty hath such grace
As I have seen in one autumnal face."

The entire poem is a monody on the encroachments of years, and neatly chronological:

"If we love things long-sought, age is a thing
Which we are fifty years in compassing;
If transitory things, which soon decay,
Age must be loveliest at the latest day."

It strikes the modern ear as maladroit enough that a woman in her yet sunshiny forties, and a most comely woman to boot, should have required prosody's ingenious excuses for wrinkles and kindred damages. Was life so hard as that in "the spacious days"? Shakespeare, in agreement with Horace, had already reminded his handsome " Will " of the pitiless and too expeditious hour,

"When forty winters shall besiege thy brow,
And dig deep trenches in thy beauty's field!"

which also seems, to a nice historical sense, somewhat staggering. The close of Donne's little homily is perfect, and full of the winning melancholy which was part of his birthright in art, whenever he allowed himself direct and homely expression :

"May still
My love descend! and journey down the hill,
Not panting after growing beauties; so
I shall ebb on with them who homeward go."

Such was John Donne's first known tribute to his friend. She must have been early and thoroughly familiar with his manuscripts, which were passed about freely, Dr. Grosart thinks, prior to 1613, and which burned what Massinger would call " no adulterate incense " to herself. Her bays are to be gleaned off many a tree, and she must have cast a frequent influence on Donne's work, which is not traceable now. He seems to have had a Crashaw-like devotion to the Christian saint whose inheritance

"Bethina was, and jointure Magdalo,"

not unconnected with the fact that some one else was Magdalen also; never does he tire of dwelling on the coincidence and the difference. In one of his quaintly moralizing songs, he goes seeking a "true-love" primrose, where but on Montgomery Hill! for he is hers, by all chivalrous tokens, as much as he may be. Again he cites, and almost with humor:

"that perplexing eye
Which equally claims love and reverence."

And his platonics make their honorable challenge at the end of some fine lines:

"So much do I love her choice, that I
Would fain love him that shall be loved of her!"

There was prescience in that couplet. As early, at least, as 1607-8, the widow's long privacy ended, probably while she was at her "howse at Charing Cross," watching over the progress of her son George at

Westminster School; and he that was "loved of her" was the grandson of the last Lord Latimer of the Nevilles, junior brother of a nobleman who perished with Essex in 1602, and brother and heir of that Sir Henry Danvers who was created Earl of Danby in 1625 for his services in Ireland, and who literally left a green memory as the founder of the pleasant Physic Gardens at Oxford. The name of Danvers, the kindly step-father, is one of the noteworthy omissions of Lord Herbert of Cherbury's *Autobiography*. But George Herbert was devoted to him, as his many letters show, and turned to him, never in vain, during his restless years at Cambridge; and into his circle of relatives, with romantic suddenness, he afterwards married. Sir John Danvers, of Dauntsey, Wilts, was twenty years younger than his wife. It is worth while to quote the very deft and courtly statement of the case made at the last by Dr. Donne: "The natural endowments of her person were such as had their part in drawing and fixing the affections of such a person as by his birth and youth and interest in great favors at court, and legal proximity to great possessions in the world, might justly have promised him acceptance in what family soever, or upon what person soever, he had directed.... He placed them here, neither diverted thence, nor repented since. For as the well-tuning of an instrument makes higher and lower strings of one sound, so the inequality of their years was thus reduced to an evenness, that she had a cheerfulness agreeable to his youth, and he had a sober staidness conformable to her more advanced years. So that I would not consider her at so much more than forty, nor him at so much less than thirty, at that time; but as their persons were made one and their fortunes made one by marriage, so I would put their years into one number, and finding a sixty between them, think them thirty apiece; for as twins of one hour they lived."*

* Dr. Donne's conceit about the ages of his friends is better handled in the young Cartwright's

"Chloe, why wish you that your years,"

a little later. It is not impossible that Cartwright, an

In the August of 1607, a masque by John Marston was given in the now ruined castle of Ashby-de-la-Zouch, eighteen miles from Leicester, as an entertainment devised by Lord Huntingdon and his young wife, the Lady Elizabeth Stanley, to welcome her mother, Alice, Countess-Dowager of Derby,* "the first night of her honor's arrival at the house of Ashby." Fourteen noble ladies took part in the masque, and among them was " Mris Da'vers." The name may, perhaps, be recognized as that of the subject of this sketch, for Sir John Danvers was not knighted until the following year; and it has been so recognized by interested

Oxonian and an observer, may have drawn upon Donne's report of this very wedding for his charming and ingenious lyric.

* This august personage was one of the Spencers of Althorp. At this time she had been for six years the wife of her second husband, the Lord Keeper Egerton, although retaining the magnificent title of her widowhood. At their estate of Harefield in Middlesex, Milton's *Arcades* was afterwards given, and it will be remembered what fine compliments to the then aged countess-dowager figure in its opening verses. Spenser's *Teares of the Muses* had been dedicated to her, in her prime, and she was the Amaryllis "highest in degree" of his *Colin Clout's Come Home Again.*

scholars who have searched Nichols's *Progresses of James I*. And yet we cannot be too sure that we have her before us, in the wreaths and picturesque draperies of the amateur stage; for there was another Mistress Da'vers at court, whose purported letter, dated February 3, 1613, signed with her confusing Christian names of "Mary Magdaline," gave great trouble, thirty years ago, to the experts of the Camden Society. Besides, a letter of the good gossipy Chamberlain, dated March 3, 1608-9, mentions as if it were then a piece of fresh news: "Young Davers is likewise wedded to the widow Herbert, Sir Edward's mother, of more than twice his age." This would seem to preclude the possibility of the fair masquer being the same person.

The mother of many Herberts, the "more than forty" bride, was by nature a home-keeping character. Among the correspondence relating to Lord Herbert of Cherbury, privately printed in 1886 by the Earl of Powis, are a few pages which give us invaluable glimpses of the London household. Lady Danvers's eldest

son, who set off upon his travels soon
after her second marriage, and who applied
himself vigorously to the various diver-
sions of body and mind catalogued in
the *Autobiography*, found himself often
pinched for money. In such a strait, not
unfamiliar to other fine gentlemen of his
day, he invariably appealed to the services of the step-father who was his junior,
in England. The latter, writing how
" wee are all some what after the olde
manner, and doe hartely wish you well,"
seems to have busied himself to some
avail, in concert with his brother-in-law,
Sir Francis Newport (the first Lord
Newport), in securing letters of credit to
Milan, Turin, the Netherlands, and elsewhere, and in explaining at length, in his
long involved sentences, how matters
could be bettered. Whether or not the
absent Knight of the Bath had reason
to suspect Sir John's disinterested action
when it came to the handling of pounds
and pence, he does not seem, then or
after, to have burdened him with any
great harvest of thanks. But Sir John's
faithful wife knew how to defend him, in

a script of May 12, 1615, which may be quoted precisely as it stands in the Herbert papers.

"To my best beloved sonn, S'r Edward Herbert, Knight,
"My deare Sonn,
it is straunge to me to here you to complayne of want of care of you in your absence when my thoughts are seldom removed from you which must assuredly set me aworkinge of any thinge may doe you good, & for writinge the one of us yf not both never let messenges pass without letter, your stay abroad is so short in any one place & we so unhappy in givinge you contentment as our letters com not to your hands which we are sorry for. And to tel you further of S'r John Da'vers Love which I dare sweare is to no man more, he is & hath beene so careful to keep you from lake of money now you are abroad as your Baylife faylinge payment as they continually doe & pay no man, he goeth to your Merchaunt, offers him self & all the powers he can make to supply you as your occasions may require, mistake him not, but beleeve me there was never a tenderer hart or a lovinger minde in any man then is in him towards you who have power to com'aund him & all that is his.

Now for your Baylifs I must tell you they have not yet payed your brothers all their Anuities due at Midsom'er past & but half due at Christmas last and no news of the rest, this yf advauntage were taken might be preiuditiall to you and it is ill for your Brothers & very ill you have such officers.

"I hope it will bringe you home & that is all the good can com of this. your sister Johnes hath long beene sicke & within this 8 dayes hath brought a boy she is so weake as she is much feared by those aboute her. my Lady Vachell lyes now adyeinge the bell hath twice gone for her. your wife & sweet children are well & herein I send you little Florence letter to see what comfort you may have of your deare children. let them, my Dear sonn, draw you home & affoorde them your care and me your comfort that desire more to see you then I desire any thinge ells in the world. and now I end with my dayly prayer for your health and safe retorne to Your ever lovinge mother, Magd : Da'vers.

"I have received the Pattent of your Br: William, & S'r John hath beene with the ambassatore who stayes for S'r James Sandaline * his cominge."

* Sir James Sandelyn, Sandalo, or Sandilands (who

A sympathizing reader, aware of sequences, may wonder whence Sir John drew "all the powers he can make"! The dignified letter, with its undulating syntax and thrifty punctuation, harmonizes with all we know of this delightful woman, who could so reproach what she deemed a shortcoming, without a touch of temper. How affectionate is the reference to the "little Florence" who died young, and to the other children, sufficiently precious to all that household, except to the wool-gathering chevalier their father, far away! Their innocent faces peer again through a sweet postscript of their grand-uncle: ("Dick is here, Ned and Bettye at Haughmond,") written in the winter, from Eyton, to the truant at

---

cuts his finest figure as Jacobus Sandilandius in *The Muses' Welcome*) was appointed Maistre d'Hostel to the beloved and beautiful Princess Elizabeth on her marriage to Frederic, Count Palatine of the Rhine, afterwards King of Bohemia, in 1612. As Sir James's name is down on the lists of the Exchequer for a gift in 1615, and as his little son Richard was baptized in Deptford Church two months after the date of Lady Danvers's letter, we may conclude that he came back to England just when the "ambassatore" expected him.

the Hague.* This same genial Sir Francis Newport, "imoderately desyring to see you," confides to his nephew, during what he complains of as "a verye drye and hott time"† for Shropshire farmers, that "mye syster your mother is confident to take a iourney into these pts this somer, the rather, I think, because yo'r brother Vaugh'n is dead & if yo' have a willing harte you maye come tyme enough to acco'pany her heare, & would not then the companye bee much the better?" But we fear the little excursion never came off. Edward Herbert's next visit to his home, presumably after a four-years' absence, was in 1619; and in May of that year he accepted the office of Ambassador to France, and spread his

* Edward Herbert served as a volunteer in the campaign of 1614-15 in the Netherlands, under the Prince of Orange. Richard Herbert, here mentioned, was his eldest son, a future Cavalier and captain of a troop of horse in the Civil Wars; Edward was the baby, and "Bettye" the child Beatrice, destined, like her sister, to a short life.

† This 1614-15 was an eccentric and un-English year throughout. The winter signalized itself by the Great Snow; "*frigus intensum,*" as Camden says, "*et nix copiosissima.*"

ready wing again to the Continent. And the *Athenæ Oxoniensis* will not let us forget that the too spirited envoy had to be temporarily recalled in 1621, because he had "irreverently treated" De Luynes, the powerful but good-for-nothing Constable of France. It is not insignificant that this was the year in which George Herbert wrote to his mother in one of his consoling moods, bidding her be of good cheer, albeit her health and wealth were gone, and the conduct of her children was not very satisfying!

We know that Lady Danvers had the "honor, love, obedience, troops of friends" which became her, and that she lost none of her influence, none of her serene charm. Her poet was much with her in his advancing age. In July, 1625, while the plague was raging in London, Donne reminded Sir Henry Wotton of the leisure he enjoyed, golden as Cicero's, by dating his letter "from S'r John Davor's house at Chelsey, of w'ich house & my Lord Carlil's at Hanworth I make up my Tusculum." Many a peaceful evening must they have passed upon the terraces, with-

in sound of the solemn songs always dear
to both. Visitors yet more illustrious
came there from the city; for the noble
hostess had once the privilege of reviv-
ing the great Lord Bacon,* who had faint-
ed in her garden. We learn, with sympathy, that "sickness, in the declination
of her years, had opened her to an over-
flowing of melancholy; not that she ever
lay under that water, but yet had, sometimes, some high tides of it." Death
chose Dr. Donne's ministering angel before him, after thirty years of mutual
fealty. Her restless son Edward, now at
home, was already eminent, and wearing
his little Irish title of Baron Castleisland;
her thoughtful Charles was long dead;
her brother, also, was no more; her
daughters were matrons, and dwelling in
prosperity. With but one unfulfilled wish,
that of seeing her favorite George married and in holy orders,† and after a life

---

* Lord Bacon dedicated to Edward Herbert, "the father of English deists," his very flat translation of the
Psalms! George wrote three Latin poems in his honor,
one being upon the occasion of his death.

† He was, in July of 1626, ordained deacon, and preb-

which left a wake of sunshine behind it in the world, very patiently and hopefully Magdalen Newport, Lady Danvers, entered upon eternity, in the early June of 1627. On the eighth day of the month, in St. Luke's, the parish church of Chelsea, she was buried:

"Old age with snow-bright hair, and folded palm,"

the final earthly glimpse of her still traditionally beautiful. On the first of July her faithful liegeman, now Dean of St. Paul's and Vicar of St. Dunstan-in-the-West, preached her funeral sermon there, before a crowd of the great ones of London, the clergy, and the poor. Izaak Walton's kind face looked up from a near pew, whence he saw Dr. Donne's tears, and felt his breaking voice, the voice of one who did not belie his friend, nigh the end of his own pilgrimage. In present grief and among graver memories, he had the true perception not to forget how joyous she had been. "She died," he said,

endary of Layton Ecclesia in Huntingdonshire. Readers of Walton will remember how his dear mother invited him to commit simony on that occasion.

"without any change of countenance or posture, without any struggling, any disorder, . . . and expected that which she hath received : God's physic and God's music, a Christianly death. . . . She was eyes to the blind, and feet to the lame, . . . naturally cheerful and merry, and loving facetiousness and sharpness of wit." His own fund of mirth and strength was fast going ; and a haunting line of his youth,

"And all my pleasures are like yesterday,"

must have reverted to him many and many a time. Morbid and persistent thoughts beset him from this hour, probably, more than ever, until he had the effigy of himself, painted as he was, laid in his failing sight ;* morbid and persistent thoughts of the ruin which befalls the bright bodies of humanity, sometimes

* The standing marble figure in a winding-sheet which Dr. King had modelled upon this strange painting on wood, may yet be seen in the south ambulatory of the choir of St. Paul's ; almost the only relic saved from the old cathedral which perished in the Great Fire of 1666. It is not only of unique interest, but of considerable artistic beauty, and " seems to breathe faintly," as Sir Henry Wotton said of it.

surging up in his loneliness, and crowding out the better vision which yet may "grace us in the disgrace of death." His inward eye was drawn strongly to his friend's sepulchre, sealed and sombre before him, and to what had been her, "going into dust now almost a month of days, almost a lunar year.... which, while I speak, is mouldering and crumbling into less and less dust." But he ended in a wholesomer strain, subdued and calm: " This good soul being thus laid down to sleep in His peace, 'I charge you, O daughters of Jerusalem, that ye wake her not!'"

The rare little duodecimo which contains Lady Danvers's funeral sermon was printed soon after, "together with other Commemorations of Her, by her Sonne G. Herbert," and offered to the public at the Golden Lion in Paul's Churchyard. The commemorations are in Greek and Latin. Strangely enough, nowhere is the sweet and sage poet of *The Temple* so set upon his prosody, so given to awkward pagan conceits, so out of tune with the ideals of classic diction. But he, who tenderly loved his mother, has given to us, in the *Memoriæ Matris Sacrum*, several precious personal fragments, and one more precious whole picture of daily habits in the lines beginning *Corneliæ sanctæ:* her morning prayer, her bath, and the plaiting of her glossy hair; her housewifely cares, her fit replies, her writing to her friends, her passion for music, her gentle helpfulness; the long felicity of a glad and stainless life,

"Quicquid habet tellus, quicquid et astra, fruens."

Dr. Donne died in 1631, whatever was yet of earth in his spirit healed and chastened by long pain. His last remembrance to some he loved was his own seal of Christ on the Anchor, "engraven very small on heliotropium stones, and set in gold, for rings." Many of those to whom his heart would have turned, the "autumnal beauty" scarce second among them, had preceded him out of England. But in travelling towards his Maker, he had that other sacred hope to "ebb on with them," and gloriously overtake them, as he traced the epitaph which covered him in old St. Paul's: "*Hic licet in occiduo cinere, aspicit eum cujus nomen est Oriens.*" The tie between himself and her was not unremembered in the next generation; for we find John Donne the younger dedicating his father's posthumous work to Francis, Lord Newport, and when making his will, in 1662, bequeathing also to the same Lord Newport "the picture of St. Anthony in a round frame." And thus, in a revived fragrance, the annals of true friendship close.

These rapid, ragged strokes of a pen make the only possible biography of Lady Danvers. When Walton wrote of her, he had the entire correspondence with Dr. Donne before him.* "There were sacred endearments betwixt these two excellent persons," he assures us, but disappointingly hurries on into the highway of his subject. It is curious that it seems impossible now to trace these breathing relics, or others from the same source;

* Dr. Donne's papers were bequeathed to Dr. Henry King, the poet-Bishop of Chichester, then residentiary of St. Paul's. The "find" were a precious one, if they yet survive.

for George Herbert, in the second elegy of the *Parentalia*, has much to say, and very sweetly, of the industry of his mother's "white right hand," and of the "many and most notable letters, flying over all the world." Much detail is utterly lost which men who agree with Prosper Mérimée that all Thucydides would not be worth an authentic memoir of Aspasia, or even of one of the slaves of Pericles, might be glad to remember. A copy of a song, a reminiscence of the glow and stir of the days through which she moved, a guess through a mist at the blond head,* the half-imperious carriage, the open hand, as she went her ways, like Dante's lovely lady, *sentendosi laudare,—* these are all we have of the daughter of England's golden age. It would be easy,

---

* The half-romantic reference, which occurs more than once in Donne's poems, to his own long-dead arm which still shall keep

"The bracelet of bright hair about the bone,"—

has it nothing to do with this blond head? *Honi soit qui mal y pense.* The internal evidences in *The Relic*, with its mention of St. Mary Magdalen, and its boast of purest friendship, and the roguery of the closing line in *The Funeral*, are somewhat strong, nevertheless.

were it also just, to throw a dash of color into her shadowy history. One would like to verify the scene at Eyton, while the news of the coming Armada roused the lion in Drake, and struck terror into the Devon towns; and to hear the young wife, with three lisping Herberts at her knee, beguile them with mellow contralto snatches of a Robin Hood ballad, or with the sweet yesterday's tale of Zutphen, where their country's dearest gave his cup of water to a dying comrade. A decade later, before their handsome bluff father, her other healthful boys stood up to wrestle, and twang their arrows at forty paces; or a rosy daughter stole to his side, and asked him of mishaps in Ireland, or of the giant laughter bubbling from the "oracle of Apollo" in a London street. It is to be believed that one who watched events through the insurrection of Essex, through Raleigh's dramatic trial, reprieve, and execution, through the national mourning for the Prince of Wales, through the fever for colonization, the savage sea-fights, the great intrigues in behalf of the Queen of Scots, the religious divisions, the muttering parliamentary thunders, the stress and heat of the exciting dawn of the seventeenth century, was not unmindful of all it meant to be alive, there and then. Magdalen Newport's girlhood fell on Lyly's *Euphues*, fresh from the printers; the *Arcadia* made the talk of Oxford, in her prime; the dusky splendor of Marlowe's *Faustus* was abroad before her second marriage. She was, surely, aware of Shakespeare, and of the wonder-folio of 1623; of the newest delighting madrigals and antiphons set forth by one Robert Jones, when every soul in England had the gift of music; of rascal Robert Greene's lovable lyrics, of Wyatt's, Campion's, and Drayton's. She wrote no verses, indeed, but her familiars wrote them; her every step jostled a Muse. We may assume that no growth nor loss in literary circles escaped that tender "perplexing eye." Perhaps it glistened from a bench, in the pioneer British theatre, on the actors of *Volpone*, and followed silently, behind the royal group, the first mincings of the first dear Fool in *King Lear*, one day-after-

Christmas at Whitehall. Last of all, for whim's sake, how any sociologist would enjoy having the honest opinion of young Lady Herbert, or that of little Mistress Donne, concerning the person they could but thank and praise! *Utinam vivisset Pepys!* It is a cheat of history that it preserves no clearer tint or trace of this chosen passer-by. Such, in truth, she was, and the quiet vanishing name clings to her: the woman of durable gladness, happily born and taught, like the soul whereof Sir Henry Wotton, who must have known her well, made his immortal song.

Of the gracious figure of Sir John Danvers we may be said to lose sight; for he seems less gracious, as by a Hindoo trick, as soon as it is written that his wife departed unto her reward. Comment on his character is equal comment upon hers, and adds new force to the classic episode of a lady philanthropist espousing a ne'er-do-weel and a featherbrain. Aubrey, always happy over a little ultra-contemporary gossip, calls it " a disagreeable match," disappointing to the bridegroom's kindred; but adds that " he married her for love of her wit." Now, wit is an admirable magnet, but it is to be suspected that there was also, and in the immediate vicinity, "metal more attractive," as Hamlet says. In the Chelsea parish-books is an entry, the first of its kind, certifying that Sir John Danvers had settled his account with "the poore," a matter of thirty pounds' loan (in which the vicar must have connived), for the year ending in January of 1628. If the payment were, by any hap, in advance, it may have fallen in Lady Danvers's own lifetime; and if so, it is quite as likely that she paid it, with an admonition! Her "high tides of melancholy," of whose true cause she certainly would not have complained to Dr. Donne, had something to do with this young spendthrift, who must have had his wheedling way, sooner or later, with such of her ample revenues as were yet extant. Perhaps Lord Herbert of Cherbury was both shrewd and charitable, in suppressing mention of his new relative.* The

* The famous *Autobiography*, indeed, boldly assures posterity that Lady Herbert, after 1597, "continued un-

longer one looks into the matter, the less curious seems his unexplained silence concerning this late graft of a family hitherto always respectable and always loyal.

There are gleams of subsequent private history in the tell-tale records at Chelsea. We are not incurably astonished to learn that as early as May of 1629 was christened Elizabeth, daughter of Sir John Danvers and Elizabeth his wife. This Lady Elizabeth, arriving providentially with her Dauntsey wealth, having borne him four children, died, as did his mother, in 1636; and left him even as she found him, none too monogamous. In 1648 Sir John Danvers again appeared at the venerable altars where his first saint never had a memorial, loving, honoring, and cherishing a Mrs. Grace Hewes, Hawes, or Hewet, of Kemerton in Gloucestershire, and, as it is to be surmised, lead-

married," and, in brief, "was the woman Dr. Donne hath described her." The acknowledgment of the accuracy of that funeral sermon, containing, as it does, its very specific Danvers passages, is in our fearless philosopher's best style.

ing her tame fortune by a ribbon. His debts and difficulties, not of one but of all time, sprout perennially in the registers. His indefatigable name, oftener than any rival's whatsoever, figures as borrowing and paying interest on a forty-pound note, which, like a Hydra-head, was always forthcoming so soon as it was demolished. This disgraceful business was the man's chief concern: for the older he grew the deeper and deeper he sank into entanglements, particularly after the death of the King. It was never doubted, in his day, but that this was a judgment on the former Gentleman Usher who affixed hand and seal to the warrant of his sovereign's execution.* His own family, it is said, as well as the royalist Herberts and Newports, dropped his acquaintance; and who knows whether Mrs. Grace Hewet was faithful? At his favorite Chelsea, in the April of 1655, and in about the seventy-

---

* There was afterwards, in France, a Gentleman of the Bedchamber who had other notions. "Gratitude," said Thierry to his executioner in the court-yard of the Abbaye—"gratitude has no opinions. I am leal to my master."

fourth year of his age, Sir John Danvers ended his career by more conventional agencies than the rope and the knife, which might have befallen him in the Stuart triumph of the morrow. His manor fell an immediate forfeit to the crown. In 1661, the dead republican was attainted, and all of his estate which was unprotected was declared regal booty. The year before his own burial at Dauntsey he laid there, "to the great grief of all good men," the body of his elder son Henry, who had just attained his majority. The Earl of Danby had died, "full of honors, wounds, and days," in 1643, while this Henry, his nephew, was still a hopeful child; and on him alone he had taken pains to settle his possessions. But Henry, in turn, was persuaded to bequeath the major part of them to his father's ever-gaping pocket, the remainder reverting to one of his two surviving sisters. The third Lady Danvers, who lived until 1678, had also a son Charles,* who petitioned the crown for his paternal rights, but

* An elder Charles, son of the Lady Elizabeth Danvers, was baptized in 1632, and must have died early.

died in old age, with neither income nor issue.

Clarendon quietly indicts Sir John Danvers as a "proud, formal, weak man," such as Cromwell "employed and contemned at once." George Bate gives him a harder character, saying that he "proved his brother to be a delinquent in the Rump Parliament, whereby he might overthrow his will, and so compass the estate himself. He sided with the sectarian party, was one of the King's judges, and lived afterwards some years in his sin, without repentance." But the same accuser adds the saving fact that Dr. Thomas Fuller, like Aubrey, was Sir John's friend, and, by his desire, preached many times at Chelsea, "where, I am sure, he was instructed to repent of his misguided and wicked consultations in having to do with the murther of that just man." One half surmises that had the preliminaries of the great struggle occurred in her time Magdalen Herbert's rather austere and advanced standards of right would have stood it out, despite her traditions, for the Commons against

Carolus Agnus.* But that would have been a very different matter from sharing the feelings of the crude advocates of revolution and regicide. What a misconception of her spotless motives must she have borne, had others found her in agreement with her vagabond lord, who treated politics as he treated the sacrament of matrimony, purely as a makeshift and a speculation!

He was no raw-head-and-bloody-bones, this Roderigo - like Briton who won the approval of Lord Bacon, and whom George Wither thanks for "those pleasurable refreshments often vouchsafed"; and whom very different men, such as George Herbert and Walton † and peaceable Fuller loved. He was a comely creature of

---

* Edward Herbert sided eventually with the Parliament, which indemnified him for the burning and sacking of Montgomery Castle.

† The six very innocent, cheerful, pious ten-syllable stanzas, attributed in *The Complete Angler* to "another angler, Jo. Davors, Esq.," are not, it is hardly necessary to add, from our scapegrace's pen. He ceased to be " Jo. Davors, Esq.," when Walton was fourteen years old.

some parts, a luckless worldling anxious to feather his own nest, and driven by timidity and the desire of gain into treacheries against himself. His short, thin, and "fayre bodie," common, as George Herbert would have us imply, to all who bore his name, his elegance, his hospitality, and his devotedness to his elderly wife, carried him off handsomely in the eyes of her jealous circle. His house in Chelsea, commemorated now by Danvers Street, adjoined that which had been Sir Thomas More's, and was presumably a part of the same estate. All around it, and due to its master's genuine enthusiasm, lay the first Italian garden planted in England; and there, rolling towards the Thames, were the long glowing flower-beds and green orchard-alleys, which were also the "*horti deliciæ dominæ*" recalled thrice in the music of filial sorrow. This home of Magdalen Danvers was pulled down, and built over, in 1716. Within its unfallen walls, where she spent her serene married life, and where she died, she had time to think, nevertheless, that she stood, towards evening, in the ways of folly, and that hers was one of those little incipient domestic tragedies which must always look amusing, even to a friend.

II
HENRY VAUGHAN
1621-1695

HENRY VAUGHAN

ON his own person, Henry Vaughan left no trace in society. His life seemed to slip by like the running water on which he was forever gazing and moralizing, and his memory met early with the fate which he hardly foresaw. Descended from the royal chiefs of southern Wales whom Tacitus mentions, and whose abode, in the day of Roman domination, was in the district called Siluria,* he called himself the Silurist upon his title-pages; and he keeps the distinctive name in the humblest of epitaphs, close by his home in the glorious valley of the Usk and the little Honddu, under the shadow of Tretower, the ruined castle of his race, and of Pen-y-

* Siluria comprised the shires of Monmouth, Hereford, Glamorgan, Radnor, and Brecon.

Fan and his kindred peaks. What we know of him is a sort of pastoral: how he was born, the son of a poor gentleman, in 1621, at Newton St. Bridget, in the old house yet asleep on the road between Brecon and Crickhowel; how he went up to Oxford, Laud's Oxford, with Thomas, his twin, as a boy of sixteen, to be entered at Jesus College;* how he took his degree (just where and when no one can discover), and came back, after a London revel, to be the village physician, though he was meant for the law, in what had become his brother's parish of Llansaintfraed; to write books full of sequestered beauty, to watch the most tragic of wars, to look into the faces of love and loss, and to spend his thoughtful age on the bowery banks of the river he had always known, his *Isca parens florum*, to

* The Reverend H. F. Lyte, Vaughan's enthusiastic editor, best known as the author of *Abide with Me*, reminds us that there was another Henry Vaughan of the same college and the same neighborhood at home—a pleasant theological person not to be confounded with the poet. It was probably he, and not the Silurist, who devoted some verses to Charles the First in the book called *Eucharistica Oxoniensis*, 1641.

which he consecrated many a sweet English line. And the ripple of the not unthankful Usk was "distinctly audible over its pebbles," as was the Tweed to the failing sense of Sir Walter, in the room where Henry Vaughan drew his last breath, on St. George's day, April 23, 1695. He died exactly seventy-nine years after Shakespeare, exactly one hundred and fifty-five years before Wordsworth.

Circumstances had their way with him, as with most poets. He knew the touch of disappointment and renunciation, not only in life, but in his civic hopes and in his art. He broke his career in twain, and began over, before he had passed thirty; and he showed great æsthetic discretion, as well as disinterestedness, in replacing his graceful early verses by the deep dedications of his prime. Religious faith and meditation seem so much part of his innermost nature, it is a little difficult to remember that Vaughan considered himself a brand snatched from the burning, a lawless Cavalier brought by the best of chances to the quiet life, and the feet of the moral Muse. He suffered most of the time between 1643 and 1651 from a sorely protracted and nearly fatal illness; and during its progress his wife and his dearest friends were taken from him. Nor was the execution of the King a light event to so sensitive a poet and so passionate a partisan. Meanwhile Vaughan read George Herbert, and his theory of proportional values began to change. It was a season of transition and silent crises, when men bared their breasts to great issues, and when it was easy for a childlike soul,

> "Weary of her vain search below, above,
> In the first Fair to find the immortal Love."*

Vaughan, in his new fervor, did his best to suppress the numbers written in his youth, thus clearing the field for what he afterwards called his "hagiography"; and a critic may wonder what he found in his first tiny volume of 1646, or in *Olor Iscanus*, to regret or cancel. Every unbaptized song is "bright only in its own

---

* These deep Augustinian lines are Carew's, gay Carew's; and they mark the highest religious expression of their time.

innocence, and kindles nothing but a generous thought"; and one of them, at least, has a manly postlude of love and resolve worthy of the free lyres of Lovelace and Montrose. Vaughan, unlike other ardent spirits of his class, had nothing very gross to be sorry for; if he was, indeed, one of his own

> "feverish souls,
> Sick with a scarf or glove,"

he had none but noble ravings. Happily, his very last verses, *Thalia Rediviva*, breaking as it were by accident a silence of twenty-three years, indorse with cheerful gallantry the accents of his youth. The turn in his life which brought him lasting peace, in a world rocking between the cant of the Parliament and resurgent audacity and riot, achieved for us a body of work which, small as it is, has rare interest, and an out-of-door beauty, as of the natural dusk, "breathless with adoration," which is almost without parallel. Eternity has been known to spoil a poet for time, but not in this instance. Never did religion and art interchange a more fortunate service, outside Italian studios. Once he had shaken off secular ambitions, Vaughan's voice grew at once freer and more forceful. In him a marked intellectual gain sprang from an apparently slight spiritual readjustment, even as it did, three centuries later, in one greater than he, John Henry Newman.

Vaughan's work is thickly sown with personalities, but they are so delicate and involved that there is little profit in detaching them. What record he made at the University is not apparent; nor is it at all sure that so independent and speculative a mind applied itself gracefully to the curriculum. He was, in the only liberal sense, a learned man, full of lifelong curiosity for the fruit of the Eden Tree. His lines beginning

"Quite spent with thought I left my cell"

show the acutest thirst for hidden knowledge; he would "most gladly die," if death might buy him intellectual growth. He looks forward to eternity as to the unsealing and disclosing of mysteries. He makes the soul sing joyously to the body:

"I that here saw darkly, in a glass,
 But mists and shadows pass,
And by their own weak shine did search the springs
 And source of things,
Shall, with inlighted rays,
 Pierce all their ways!"

With an imperious query, he encounters the host of midnight stars:

"Who circled in
Corruption with this glorious ring?"

What Vaughan does know is nothing to him; when he salutes the Bodleian from his heart, he is thinking how little honey he has gathered from that vast hive, and how little it contains, when measured with what there is to learn from living and dying. He had small respect for the sinister sciences among which the studies of his beloved brother, a Neo-Platonist, lay. Though he was no pedant, he dearly loved to get in a slap against the ignorant whom we have always with us. At twenty-five, he printed a good adaptation of the Tenth of Juvenal, and flourished his wit, in the preface, at the expense of some possible gentle reader of the parliamentary persuasion who would "quarrel with antiquitie." "These, indeed, may think that they have slept out so many centuries in this Satire, and are now awaked; which had it been still Latin, perhaps their nap had been everlasting!"

He was an optimist, proven through much personal trial; he had sympathy with the lower animals, and preserved a humorous deference towards all things alive, even the leviathan of Holy Writ, which he affectionately exalts into "the shipmen's fear" and "the comely spacious whale"! Vaughan adored his friends; he had a unique veneration for childhood; his adjective for the admirable and beautiful, whether material or immaterial, is "dear"; and his mind dwelt with habitual fondness on what Sir Thomas Browne (a man after his own heart) calls "incomprehensibles, and thoughts of things which thoughts do but tenderly touch."

His occupation as a resident physician

must have fostered his fine eye and ear for the green earth, and furnished him, day by day, with musings in sylvan solitudes, and rides abroad over the fresh hill-paths. The breath of the mountains is about his books. An early riser, he uttered a constant invocation to whomever would listen, that

> "Manna was not good
> After sun-rising; far-day sullies flowers."

He was hospitable on a limited income.* His verses of invitation *To his Retired Friend*, which are not without their thrusts at passing events, have a classic jollity fit to remind the reader of Randolph's ringing ode to Master Anthony Stafford. Again and again Vaughan reiterates the Socratic and Horatian song of content: that he has enough lands

---

* Vaughan apparently enjoyed that privilege of genius, acquaintance with a London garret, if we may take autobiographically the fine brag worthy of the tribe of Henri Mürger:
> "I scorn your land,
> So far it lies below me; here I see
> How all the sacred stars do circle me."

and money, that there are a thousand things he does not want, that he is blessed in what he has. All this does not prevent him from recording the phenomenal ebb-tides of his purse, and from whimsically synthesizing on "the threadbare, goldless genealogie" of bards! No sour zealot in anything, he enjoyed an evening now and then at the Globe Tavern in London, where he consumed his sack with relish, that he might be "possessor of more soul," and "after full cups have dreams poetical." But he was no lover of the town. Country life was his joy and pride; the only thing which seemed, in his own most vivid phrase, to "fill his breast with home."

> "Here something still like Eden looks!
> Honey in woods, juleps in brooks."

A literary acquaintance, one unrecognized N. W., congratulates Vaughan that he is able to "give his Muse the swing in an hereditary shade." He translated with great gusto *The Old Man of Verona*, out of Claudian, and Guevara's *Happiness of Country Life;* and he notes with satisfaction that Abraham was of his rural mind, in "Mamre's holy grove." Vaughan was an angler, need it be added? Nay, the autocrat of anglers: he was a salmon-catcher.

With "the charity which thinketh no evil," he loved almost everything, except the Jesuits, and his ogres the Puritans. For Vaughan knew where he stood, and his opinion of Puritanism never varied. He kept his snarls and satires, for the most part, hedged within his prose, the proper ground of the animosities. When he put on his singing-robes, he tried to forget, not always with success, his spites and bigotries. For his life, he could not help sidelong glances, stings, strictures between his teeth, thistle-down hints cast abroad in the neatest of generalities:

"Who saint themselves, they are no saints!"

The introduction to his *Mount of Olives* (whose pages have a soft billowy music like Jeremy Taylor's) is nominally inscribed to "the peaceful, humble, and pious reader." That functionary must have found it a trial to preserve his peaceful and pious abstraction, while the peaceful and pious author proceeded to flout the existing government, in a towering rage, and in very elegant caustic English. Vaughan was none too godly to be a thorough hater. He was genially disposed to the pretensions of every human creature; he refused to consider his ancestry and nurture by themselves, as any guarantee of the justice of his views or of his superior insight into affairs. Yet in spite of his enforced Quaker attitude during the clash of arms, he nursed in that gentle bosom the heartiest loathing of democracy, and shared the tastes of a certain clerk of the Temple "who never could be brought to write Oliver with a great O." It is fortunate that he did not spoil himself, as Wither did, upon the wheels of party, for politics were his most vehement concern. Had he been richer, as he tells us in a playful passage, nothing on earth would have kept him from meddling with national issues.

    The poets, save the greatest, Milton,

his friend Andrew Marvell, and Wither, rallied in a bright group under the royal standard. Those among them who did not fight were commonly supposed, as was Drummond of Hawthornden, to redeem their reputation by dying of grief at the overthrow of the King. Yet Vaughan did not fight, and Vaughan did not die of grief. It is so sure that he suffered some privation, and it may be imprisonment, for his allegiance, that shrewd guessers, before now, have equipped him and placed him in the ranks of the losing cause, where he might have had choice company. His generous erratic brother (a writer of some note, an alchemist, an Orientalist, a Rosicrucian, who was ejected from his vicarage in 1654, and died either of the plague, or of inhaling the fumes of a caldron, at Albury, in 1665, while the court was at Oxford)* had been a recruit, and a brave one. But Henry Vaughan explicitly tells

* The King lodged at Christchurch, the Queen and my Lady Castlemaine (together, alas!) at Merton, amid endless hawking, tennis, boating, basset, and general revelry.

us, in his *Ad Posteros*, and in a prayer in the second part of *Silex Scintillans*, that he had no personal share in the constitutional struggle, that he shed no blood. Again he cries, in a third lyric,

> "O accept
> Of his vowed heart, whom Thou hast kept
> From bloody men!"

This painstaking record of a fact by one so loyal as he goes far to prove, to an inductive mind not thoroughly familiar with his circumstances, that he considered war the worst of current evils, and was willing, for this first principle of his philosophy, to lay himself open to the charge, not indeed of cowardice (was he not a Vaughan?), but of lack of appreciation for the one romantic opportunity of his life. His withdrawal from the turmoil which so became his colleagues may seem to harmonize with his known moral courage and right sentiment; and fancy is ready to fasten on him the sad neutrality, and the passionate "ingemination" for "peace, peace," which "took his sleep from him, and would shortly break his heart," such as Clarendon tells us of in his beautiful passage touching the young Lord Falkland. But it is greatly to be feared that Vaughan, despite all the abstract reasoning which arrays itself against so babyish and barbarous a thing as a battle, would have swung himself into a saddle as readily as any, had not "God's finger touched him." A comparison of dates will show that he was bedridden, while his hot heart was afield with the shouting gentlemen whom Mr. Browning heard in a vision:

> "King Charles! and who'll do him right, now?
> King Charles! and who's ripe for fight, now?
> Give a rouse: here's in Hell's despite now,
> King Charles!"

This is the secret of Vaughan's blood-guiltlessness. Of course he thanked Heaven, after, that he was kept clean of carnage; he would have thanked Heaven for anything that happened to him. It was providential that we of posterity lost a soldier in the Silurist, and gained a poet. As the great confusion cleared, his spirit cleared too, and the Vaughan we know,

> "Delicious, lusty, amiable, fair,"

comes in, like a protesting angel, with
the Commonwealth. Perhaps he lived
long enough to sum up the vanity of
statecraft and the instability of public
choice, driven from tyranny to license,
from absolute monarchy to absolute an-
archy; and to turn once more to his
"loud brook's incessant fall" as an object much worthier of a rational man's
regard. Born while James I. was vain-
gloriously reigning, Henry Vaughan survived the Civil War, the two Protector-
ates, the orgies of the Restoration (which
he did not fail to satirize), and the Revolution of "Meenie the daughter," as the
old Scots song slyly calls her. He had
seen the Stuarts in and out, in and out
again, and his seventy-four years, on-
lookers at a tragedy, were not forced to
sit through the dull Georgian farce which
began almost as soon as his grave was
green.

Moreover, he was thoroughly out of
touch with his surroundings. While all
the world was either devil-may-care or
Calvin-colored, he had for his characteristic a rapt, inexhaustible joy, buoying

him up and sweeping him away. He might well have said, like Dr. Henry More, his twin's rival and challenger in metaphysics, that he was "most of his time mad with pleasure." While

> "every burgess foots'
> The mortal pavement in eternal boots,"

Vaughan lay indolently along a bank, like a shepherd swain, pondering upon the brood of "green-heads" who denied miracles to have been or to be, and wishing the noisy passengers on the highways of life could be taught the value of

> "A sweet self-privacy in a right soul."

His mind turned to paradoxes and inverted meanings, and the analysis of his own tenacious dreams, in an England of pikes and bludgeons and hock-carts and wassail-cakes. "A proud, humoursome person," Anthony à Wood called him. He was something of a fatalist, inasmuch as he followed his lonely and straight path, away from crowds, and felt eager for nothing but what fell into his open hands. He strove little, being convinced that temporal advantage is too often an eternal handicap. "Who breaks his glass to take more light," he reminds us, "makes way for storms unto his rest." This passive quality belongs to happy men, and Vaughan was a very happy man, thanks to the faith and will which made him so, although he had known calamity, and had failed in much. Throughout his pages one can trace the affecting struggle between things desired and things forborne. It is only a brave philosopher who can afford to pen a stanza intimate as this:

> "O Thou who didst deny to me
> The world's adored felicity!
> Keep still my weak eyes from the shine
> Of those gay things which are not Thine."

He had better possessions than glory under his hand in the health and peace of his middle age and in his cheerful home. He was twice married, and must have lost his first wife, nameless to us, but most tenderly mourned, in his twenty-ninth or thirtieth year. She seems to have been the mother of five of his six children. Vaughan was rich in friends. He had known Davenant and Cartwright, but it is quite characteristic of him that the two great authors to whom he was especially attached were Jonson and John Fletcher, both only a memory at the time of his first going to London. Of Randolph, Jonson's strong "son," who so beggared English literature by dying young in 1634, Vaughan sweetly says somewhere that he will hereafter

"Look for Randolph in those holy meads."

Mention of his actual fellow-workers is very infrequent, nor does he mention the Shakespeare who had "dwelt on earth unguessed at," and who is believed to have visited the estates of the Vaughans at Scethrog, and to have picked up the name of his merry fellow Puck from goblin traditions of the neighborhood. Vaughan followed his leisure and his preference in translating divers works of meditation, biography, and medicine, pleasing himself, like Queen Bess, with naturalizing bits of Boethius, and much from Plutarch, Ausonius, Severinus, and Claudian. He did some passages from

Ovid, but he must have felt sharply the violence done to the lyric essence in passing it ever so gently from language to language, for he lingered over Adrian's darling *Animula vagula blandula*, only to leave it alone, and to write of it as the saddest poetry that ever he met with.

Not the least of Henry Vaughan's blessings was his warm friendship with "the matchless Orinda."* This delightful Catherine Fowler married, in 1647, a stanch royalist, Mr. James Philips of Cardigan Priory, and as his bride, became what, in the Welsh solitudes, was considered "neighbor" to Vaughan, her home being distant from his just fifty miles as the crow flies. She had been, in her infancy, a prodigy of Biblical quotation, like Evelyn's little Richard, and grew up to be such another *précieuse* as Madame la Comtesse de Lafayette, *née*

---

* Orinda's own verses, scattered in manuscript among her friends, were collected and printed without her knowledge, and much against her desire, in 1663: a piece of treachery which threw her into a severe indisposition. She could therefore condole more than enough with Henry Vaughan. Friends were officious creatures in those days.

Lavergne; but we know that she was the cleverest and comeliest of good women, and Vaughan's association with her must have been a perpetual sunshine to him and his. She prefixed, after the fashion of the day, some commendatory verses to his published work. They are not only pretty, but they furnish a bit of adequate criticism. The secular Muse of the Silurist is, according to Orinda,

"Truth clothed in wit, and Love in innocence,"

and has, for her birthright, seriousness and a "charming rigour." The last two words might stand for him in the fast-coming day when nobody will have time to discuss old poets in anything but technical terms and epigrams. Orinda, with her accurate judgment, should have had a chance to talk to Mr. Thomas Campbell, who adorned his *Specimens* with the one official and truly prepositional phrase that "Vaughan was one of the harshest of writers, even of the inferior order of the school of conceit!"*

* This, to say the least, was not "pretty" of Campbell, who thought so well of the "world's grey fathers" con-

While Henry Vaughan was preparing for publication the first half of *Silex Scintillans* as the token of his arrested and uplifted youth, Rev. Mr. Thomas Vaughan, backed by a few other sanguine Oxonians, and disregardful of his twin's exaggerated remorse for the fruits of his profaner years, brought out the "formerly written and newly named" *Olor Iscanus*, over the author's head, in 1650, and gave to it a motto from the Georgics. The preface is in Eugenius Philalethes' own gallant style, and offers a haughty commendation to "beauty from the light retired." Perhaps Vaughan's earliest and most partial editor felt, like Thoreau on a certain occasion, that it were well to make an extreme statement, if only so he might make an emphatic one. He chose to supplicate the public of the Protectorate in this wise: "It was the glorious Maro that referred his legacies to the fire, and though princes are seldom executors, yet there came a Cæsar to his testament, as if the act of a poet

gregated to gaze at Vaughan's *Rainbow* that he conveyed them bodily into the foreground of his own.

could not be repealed but by a king. I am not, reader, Augustus Vindex: here is no royal rescue, but here is a Muse that deserves it. The author had long ago condemned these poems to obscurity and the consumptition of that further fate which attends it. This censure gave them a gust of death, and they have partly known that oblivion which our best labors must come to at last. I present thee, then, not only with a book, but with a prey, and, in this kind, the first recoveries from corruption. Here is a flame hath been some time extinguished, thoughts that have been lost and forgot, but now they break out again like the Platonic reminiscency. I have not the author's approbation to the fact, but I have law on my side, though never a sword: I hold it no man's prerogative to fire his own house. Thou seest how saucy I am grown, and if thou dost expect I should commend what is published, I must tell thee I cry no Seville oranges; I will not say 'Here is fine,' or 'cheap': that were an injury to the verse itself, and to the effect it can produce. Read on; and thou wilt find thy spirit engaged, not by the deserts of what we call tolerable, but by the commands of a pen that is above it." All this is uncritical, but useful and proper on the part of the clerical brother, who writes very much as Lord Edward Herbert might be supposed to write for George under like conditions; for he knew, according to an ancient adage, that there is great folly in pointing out the shortcomings of a work of art to eyes uneducated to its beauties. It was just as well to insist disproportionately upon the principle at stake, that Henry Vaughan's least book was unique and precious. He was not, like the majority of the happy lyrists of his time, a writer by accident; he was strictly a man of letters, and his sign-manual is large and plain upon everything which bears his name. He indites like a Roman, with evenness and without a superfluous syllable. One cannot italicize him; every word is a congested force, packed to bursting with meaning and insistence; the utterance of a man who has been thinking all his life upon his own chosen subjects, and who unerringly despatches a language about its business, as if he had just created it. Like Andrew Marvell's excellent father, " he never broached what he had never brewed." It follows that his work, to which second editions were wellnigh unknown, shows scarcely any variation from itself. It carries with it a testimony that, such as it stands, it is the very best its author can do. Its faults are not slips; they are quite as radical and congenital as its virtues. Vaughan (to transfer a fine phrase of Mr. W. T. Arnold) is "enamoured of perfection," but he is fully so before he makes up his mind to write, and from the first every stroke of his pen is fatal. It transfixes a noun or a verb, pins it to the page, and challenges a reformer to move or replace it. His modest Muse is as sure as Shakespeare, as nice as Pope; she is incapable of scruples and apprehensions, once she has spoken. What Vaughan says of Cartwright may well be applied to his own ·deliberate grace of diction:

> "Thou thy thoughts hast drest in such a strain
> As doth not only speak, but rule and reign."

His verses have the tone of a Vandyck portrait, with all its firm pensive elegance and lack of shadow.

Vaughan has very little quaintness, as we now understand that word, and none of the cloudiness and incorrigible grotesqueness which dominated his Alexandrian day. He has great temperance; he keeps his eye upon the end, and scarcely falls at all into "the fond adulteries of art," inversions, unscholarly compound words, or hard-driven metaphors. If he be difficult to follow, it is only because he lives, as it were, in highly oxygenated air; he is remote and peculiar, but not eccentric. His conceits are not monstrous; the worst of them proclaims:

> "Some love a rose
> In hand, some in the skin;
> But, cross to those,
> I would have mine within";

which will bear a comparison with Carew's hatched cherubim, or with that very provincialism of Herbert's which describes a rainbow as the lace of Peace's coat! Those of Vaughan's figures not drawn from the open air, where he was happiest, are, indeed, too bold and too many, and they come from strange corners: from finance, medicine, mills, the nursery, and the mechanism of watches and clocks. In no one instance, however, does he start wrong, like the great influencer, Donne, in *The Valediction*, and finish by turning such impediments as "stiff twin-compasses" into images of memorable beauty. The *Encyclopædia Britannica*, like Campbell, finds Vaughan "untunable," and so he is very often. But poets may not always succeed in metaphysics and in music too. The lute which has the clearest and most enticing twang under the laurel boughs is Herrick's, and not Donne's; Mr. Swinburne's, and not Mr. Browning's. It is to be observed that when Vaughan lets go of his regrets, his advice, and his growls over the bad times, he falls into instant melody, as if in that, and not in a rough impressiveness, were his real strength. His blessing for the river Usk flows sweetly as the tide it hangs upon:

> "Garlands, and songs, and roundelays,
> And dewy nights, and sunshine days,

> The turtle's voice, joy without fear,
> Dwell on thy bosom all the year!
> To thee the wind from far shall bring
> The odors of the scattered spring,
> And, loaden with the rich arrear,
> Spend it in spicy whispers here."

Vaughan played habitually with his pauses, and unconsciously threw the metrical stress on syllables and words least able to bear it; but no sensitive ear can be otherwise than pleased at the broken sequence of such lines as

> "these birds of light make a land glad
> Chirping their solemn matins on a tree,"

and the hesitant symbolism of

> "As if his liquid loose retinue stayed
> Lingering, and were of this steep place afraid."

The word "perspective," with the accent upon the first syllable, was a favorite with him; and Wordsworth approved of that usage enough to employ it in the majestic opening of the sonnet on King's College Chapel.* In short, if Vaughan

---

* Per'-spective was, of course, the general pronunciation from Shakespeare to Dr. Johnson, and is used with

be "untunable," it is because he never learned to distil vowels at the expense or peril of the message which he believed himself bound to deliver, even where hearers were next to none, and which he tried only to make compact and clear. His speech has a deep and free harmony of its own, to those whom abruptness does not repel; and even critics who turn from him to the masters of verbal sound may do him the parting honor of acknowledging the nature of his limitation.

> "A noble error, and but seldom made,
>   When poets are by too much force betrayed!"

Vaughan was a born observer, and in his poetry may be found the pioneer expression of the nineteenth-century feeling for landscape. His canvas is not often large; he had an indifference towards the exquisite presence of autumn, and an inland ignorance of the sea. But he

great beauty in Dryden's *Ode to the Memory of Mrs. Anne Killigrew*. But it is a characteristic word with Vaughan, and it was from Vaughan that Wordsworth took it.

could portray depth and distance at a stroke, as in the buoyant lines:

> "It was high spring, and all the way
> Primrosed, and hung with shade,"

which etches for you the whole winding lane, roofed and floored with beauty; he carries a reader over half a continent in his

> "Paths that are hidden from the vulture's eyes,"

and suspends him above man's planet altogether with his audacious eagle, to whom "whole seas are narrow spectacles," and who

> "in the clear height and upmost air
> Doth face the sun, and his dispersèd hair!"

Besides this large vision, Vaughan had uncommon knowledge how to employ detail, during the prolonged literary interval when it was wholly out of fashion. It has been the lot of the little rhymesters of all periods to deal with the open air in a general way, and to embellish their pages with birds and boughs; but it takes a true modern poet, under the influence of the Romantic revival, to sum up perfectly the ravages of wind and frost:

> "Where is the pride of summer, the green prime,
> The many, many leaves all twinkling?—Three
> On the mossed elm; three on the naked lime
> Trembling; and one upon the old oak tree";

and it takes another to give the only faithful and ideal report of a warbling which every schoolboy of the race had heard before him:

> "That's the wise thrush: he sings each song twice over,
> Lest you should think he never could recapture
> The first fine careless rapture."

That Vaughan's pages should furnish this patient specification is remarkable in a man whose mind was set upon things invisible. His gaze is upon the inaccessible ether, but he seems to detect everything between himself and heaven. He sighs over the inattentive rustic, whom, perhaps, he catches scowling by the pasture-bars of the wild Welsh downs:

> "O that he would hear
> The world read to him!"

Whatever is in that pleasant world he himself hears and sees; and his interrupted chronicle is always terse, graphic, straight from life. He has the inevitable phrase for every phenomenon, a little low-comedy phrase, sometimes, such as Shakespeare and Carew had used before him:

"Deep snow
Candies our country's woody brow."

It seems never to have entered the primitive mind of Vaughan to love, or serve, art and nature for themselves. His cue was to walk abroad circumspectly and with incessant reverence, because in all things he found God. He marks, at every few rods in the thickets, "those low violets of Thine," and the "breathing sacrifice" of earth-odors which the "parched and thirsty isle" gratefully sends back after a shower.* His prayer

---

* Vaughan had a relish for damp weather, the thing which makes the loveliness of the British isles, and which the ungrateful islanders are prone to revile. He never passes a sheet of water without looking upward for the forming cloud:

"That drowsy lake
From her faint bosom breathed thee!"

is that he may not forget that physical beauty is a great symbol, but only a symbol; a "hid ascent" through "masks and shadows" to the divine; or, as Mr. Lowell said in one of his last poems,

> "a tent
> Pitched for an Inmate far more excellent."

A humanist of the school of Assisi, Vaughan was full of out-of-door meeknesses and pieties, nowhere sweeter in their expression than in this all-embracing valedictory:

> "O knowing, glorious Spirit! when
> Thou shalt restore trees, beasts, and men,
> . . . .
> Give him among Thy works a place
> Who in them loved and sought Thy face."

He muses in the garden, at evenfall:

> "Man is such a marigold
> As shuts, and hangs the head."

Clouds, seasons, and the eternal stars are his playfellows; he apostrophizes our sister the rainbow, and reminds her of yesterday, when

> "Terah, Nahor, Haran, Abram, Lot,
> The youthful world's grey fathers, in one knot,"

lifted anxious looks to her new splendor. He is familiar with the depression which comes from boding weather, when

> "a pilgrim's eye,
> Far from relief,
> Measures the melancholy sky."

He has an artist's feeling, also, for the wrath of the elements, which inevitably hurry him on to the consummation

> "When Thou shalt spend Thy sacred store
> Of thunders in that heat,
> And low as e'er they lay before
> Thy six-days buildings beat!"

"I saw," he says, suddenly—

> "I saw Eternity the other night";

and he is perpetually seeing things almost as startling and as bright: the "edges and the bordering light" of lost infancy; the processional grandeur of old books, which he fearlessly calls

> "The track of fled souls, and their Milky Way";

and visions of the Judgment, when

> "from the right
> The white sheep pass into a whiter light."

Here the figure beautifully forecasts a famous one of Rossetti's. Light, indeed, is Vaughan's distinctive word, and the favorite source of his similes and illustrations.

If Vaughan's had not been so profoundly moral a nature, he would have lacked his picturesque sense of the general, the continuous. That shibboleth, "a primrose by the river's brim," is to him all the generations of all the yellow primroses smiling there since the Druids' day, and its mild moonlike ray reflects the hope and fear and pathos of the mortal pilgrimage that has seen and saluted it, age after age. Whatever he meets upon his walk is drowned and dimmed in a wide halo of association and sympathy. His unmistakable accent marks the opening of a little sermon called *The Timber ;* a sigh of pity, tender as a child's, over the fallen and unlovely logs:

"Sure, thou didst flourish once! and many springs
　Many bright mornings, much dew, many showers,
Passed o'er thy head; many light hearts and wings,
　Which now are dead, lodged in thy living towers."*

　* Sometimes erroneously printed "bowers."

Leigh Hunt once challenged England and America* to produce anything approaching, for music and feeling, the beauty of

> "boughs that shake against the cold,
> Bare ruined choirs, where late the sweet birds sang."

He forgot the closes of these artless lines of a minor poet; or he did not know them.

Vaughan's meek reputation began to renew itself about 1828, when four critics eminently fitted to appraise his worth were in their prime; but, curiously enough, none of these, not even the best of them, the same Charles Lamb who said a just and generous word for Wither, had the satisfaction of rescuing his sunken name. Lamb's friend, the good soul Bernard Barton, seems, however, to have known and admired his Vaughan.

* It was kind of the ever-kind Hunt to include America in his enumeration, at a time when the United States were supposed by his fellow-countrymen to have no literature at all of their own. The circumstance that his challenge appeared in the preface to *The Book of the Sonnet*, which was edited by Hunt in conjunction with an American, and published at Boston in 1868, may help to account for the mannerliness of the reference.

Eight little books, if we count the two parts of *Silex Scintillans* as one,* enclose all of the Silurist's original work. He began to publish in 1646, and he practically ceased in 1655, reappearing but in 1678 with *Thalia Rediviva*, which was

* In the *Letters and Memorials of Archbishop Trench*, vol. ii., p. 57, there is a letter bearing upon this point from Mr. Frank Millson, dated 1868, which deserves serious consideration from Vaughan's forthcoming editors. "I think," he writes the Dean, "that your supposition that the 1655 edition is the same book as the one of 1650, with a new title-page and additions, can hardly be correct, though I know that Lyte, the editor of Pickering's reprint, thinks as you do. The preface to the 1655 edition is dated September 30, 1654, and contains this passage" (not given in the *Memorials*) "which seems to me to refer to the fact of a new edition. A comparison of my two copies shows that the 1650 edition consists of half a sheet, title and dedication, and 110 pages. The second edition has title, preface, dedication, motto, the 110 pages of the first edition, with 84 pages of new matter, and a table of first lines. A noticeable thing in the arrangement is that the sheets do not begin with new printer's marks, as they might be expected to do if the second part were simply new matter added to the first volume, but begin with A, the last sheet of the former volume having ended with G. I am sorry to trouble you with these trifling details; but as Vaughan has long been a favorite author of mine, they have an interest for me, and if they help to show that he was not neglected by readers of his own time, I shall be glad."

not issued under his own supervision. It is commonly supposed that his verses were forgotten up to the date (1847) of the faulty but timely Aldine edition of the Rev. H. F. Lyte, thrice reprinted and revised since then, and until the appearance of Dr. Grosart's four inestimable quartos; but Mr. Carew Hazlitt has been fortunate enough to discover the advertisement of an eighteenth-century reprint of Vaughan. As the results of Dr. Grosart's patient service to our elder writers are necessarily semi-private, it may be said with truth that the real Vaughan is still debarred from the general reader, who is, indeed, the identical person least concerned about that state of affairs. His name is not irrecoverable nor unfamiliar to scholars.*

---

* Anthologies and cyclopædias nowadays, especially since Dr. John Brown and Principal Shairp drew attention to the Silurist in their pages, are more than likely to admit him. It was not so always. Winstanley, sharp as was his eye, let Vaughan escape him in his *Lives of the Poets*, published in 1687. He is not in the *Theatrum Poetarum*, nor in Johnson's *Lives*. He is in neither of Southey's collections. Mr. Palgrave allows him, in *The Golden Treasury*, but a song and a half; Ellis's sheaf of excellent *Specimens* of 1811 furnishes eighteen lines of a

His mind, on the whole, might pass for the product of yesterday; and he, who needs no glossary, may handsomely cede the honors of one to Mr. William Morris. It is at least certain that had Vaughan lately lifted up his sylvan voice out of

wedding blessing on the *Best and Most Accomplished Couple* apologizing for "their too much quaintness and conceit"; and in Willmott's *Sacred Poets* Vaughan occupies four pages, as against Crashaw's thirty-five, Herbert's thirty-seven, and Wither's one hundred and thirty-two. But Vaughan fares well in Dr. George Macdonald's *England's Antiphon*, and in Archbishop Trench's *Household Book*. Ward's *English Poets*, in the second volume, has a conventional selection from him, as has, at greater length, Fields' and Whipple's *Family Library of British Poetry*. There is a goodly list entered under Vaughan's name in Gilfillan's *Less-Known British Poets*, all chosen from his devotional work. Thirty-seven religious lyrics again adorn the splendid *Treasury of Sacred Song*. Vaughan's secular numbers yet await their proper bays, although a limited edition of most of them, containing a bibliography, was printed in 1893 by J. R. Tutin of Hull. Mr. Saintsbury, in his *Seventeenth Century Lyrics*, has a small and very choice group of Vaughan's songs, and Professor Palgrave, having to do with him for the third time, gives him large and cordial honor in the eleventh volume of *Y Cymmrodor*. In Emerson's *Parnassus* he appears but once. He had his most graceful and grateful American tribute when Mr. Lowell, long ago, named him in passing as "dear Henry Vaughan," in *A Certain Condescension in Foreigners*.

Brecknockshire, he would not so readily be accused of having modelled himself unduly upon George Herbert.* He has gone into eclipse behind that gracious name.

Henry Vaughan was a child of thirteen when Herbert, a stranger to him, died at Bemerton, and he read him first in the sick-chamber to which the five years' distresses of his early manhood confined him. The reading could not have been prior to 1647, for *Olor Iscanus*, Vaughan's second volume, was lying ready for the press that year, as we know from the date of its dedication to Lord Kildare Digby. As no novice poet, therefore, he fell under the spell of a sweet and elect soul, who was also a lover of vanquished royalty, a convert who had looked upon the vanities of the court and the city, a Welshman born, and not un-

---

* In one of his prefaces, Vaughan hits neatly at the crowd of Herbertists: "These aim more at verse than at perfection." Where there are noble resemblances, it is well to remember that two sides have the right to be heard. Mrs. Thoreau used to say: " Mr. Emerson imitates Henry!" And she was at least as accurate as the critics who annoyed her old age by the reversed statement.

connected with Vaughan's own ancient and patrician house. These were slight coincidences, but they served to strengthen a forming tie. The Silurist somewhere thanks Herbert's " holy ever-living lines " for checking his blood ; and it was, perhaps, the only service rendered of which he was conscious. But his endless iambics and his vague allegorical titles are cast thoroughly in the manner of Herbert, and he takes from the same source the heaped categorical epithets, the didactic tone, and the introspectiveness which are his most obvious failings. Vaughan's intellectual debt to Herbert resolves itself into somewhat less than nothing ; for in following him with zeal to the Missionary College of the Muses, he lost rather than gained, and he is altogether delightful and persuasive only where he is altogether himself. Nevertheless, a certain spirit of conformity and filial piety towards Herbert has betrayed Vaughan into frequent and flagrant imitations. It seems as if these must have been voluntary, and rooted in an intention to enforce the same truths in all but the same words; for the moment Vaughan breaks into invective, or comes upon his distinctive topics, such as childhood, natural beauty (for which Herbert had an imperfect sense), friendship, early death, spiritual expectation, he is off and away, free of any predecessor, thrilling and unforgettable. Comparisons will not be out of place here, for Vaughan can bear, and even invoke them. Dryden said in Jonson's praise that he was "a learned plagiary," and nobody doubts nowadays that Shakespeare and Milton were the bandit kings of their time. There was, indeed, in English letters, up to Queen Anne's reign, an open communism of ideas and idioms astonishing to look upon; there is less confiscation at present, because, outside the pale of the sciences, there is less thinking. If any one thing can be closer to another, for instance, than even Drummond's sonnet on *Sleep* is to Sidney's, it is the dress of Vaughan's morality to that of George Herbert's. Mr. Simcox is the only critic who has taken the trouble to contrast them, and he does so in so random a fashion as to suggest that his scrutiny, in some cases, has been confined to the rival titles. It is certain that no other mind, however bent upon identifications, can find a likeness between *The Quip* and *The Queer*, or between *The Tempest* and *Providence*. Vaughan's *Mutiny*, like *The Collar*, ends in a use of the word "child," after a scene of strife; and if ever it were meant to match Herbert's poem, distinctly falls behind it, and deals, besides, with a much weaker rebelliousness. *Rules and Lessons* is so unmistakably modelled upon *The Church Porch* that it scarcely calls for comment. Herbert's admonitions, however, are continued, but nowhere repeated; and Vaughan's succeed in being poetic, which the others are not. Beyond these replicas, Vaughan's structural genius is in no wise beholden to Herbert's. But numerous phrases and turns of thought descend from the master to the disciple, undergoing such subtle and peculiar changes, and given back, as Coleridge would say, with such "usurious interest," that it may well be submitted whether, in this casual list, every borrowing, save two, be not a bettering.

HERBERT.

"A throbbing conscience, spurrèd by remorse,
    Hath a strange force."

"My thoughts are all a case of knives,
    Wounding my heart
    With scattered smart."

"And trust
Half that we have
Unto an honest faithful grave."

"Teach me Thy love to know,
  That this new light which now I see
May both the work and workman show:
  Then by a sunbeam I will climb to Thee!"

"I will go searching, till I find a sun
    Shall stay till we have done,
A willing shiner, that will shine as gladly
    As frost-nipt suns look sadly.
Then we will sing and shine all our own day,
    And one another pay;
His beams shall cheer my breast, and both so twine
Till even his beams sing, and my music shine."

(Of prayer.)

"Heaven in ordinary, man well-drest,
  The Milky Way, the bird of Paradise."

"Then went I to a garden, and did spy
    A gallant flower,
The crown-imperial: Sure, said I,
    Peace at the root must dwell."

VAUGHAN.

"A darting conscience, full of stabs and fears."

"And wrap us in imaginary flights
Wide of a faithful grave."

"That in these masks and shadows I may see
Thy sacred way,
And by these hid ascents climb to that day
Which breaks from Thee
Who art in all things, though invisibly!"

"O would I were a bird or star
Fluttering in woods, or lifted far
Above this inn
And road of sin!
Then either star or bird would be
Shining or singing still to Thee!"

(*Of books.*)

"The track of fled souls, and their Milky Way."

"I walked the other day to spend my hour
Into a field,
Where I sometime had seen the soil to yield
A gallant flower."

HERBERT.

"But groans are quick and full of wings,
    And all their motions upward be,
And ever as they mount, like larks they sing:
    The note is sad, yet music for a king."

"Joys oft are there, and griefs as oft as joys,
    But griefs without a noise;
Yet speak they louder than distempered fears:
    What is so shrill as silent tears?"

"At first Thou gavest me milk and sweetnesses,
    I had my wish and way;
My days were strewed with flowers and happiness;
    There was no month but May."

    "Only a scarf or glove
Doth warm our hands, and make them write of Love."

"I got me flowers to strew Thy way,
    I got me boughs off many a tree;
But Thou wast up by break of day,
    And brought Thy sweets along with Thee."

"O come! for Thou dost know the way:
    Or if to me Thou wilt not move,
Remove me where I need not say,
    'Drop from above.'"

"Sure Thou wilt joy by gaining me
    To fly home like a laden bee."

VAUGHAN.

"A silent tear can pierce Thy throne
When loud joys want a wing;
And sweeter airs stream from a groan
Than any artèd string."

"Follow the cry no more! There is
An ancient way,
All strewed with flowers and happiness,
And fresh as May!"

"feverish souls
Sick with a scarf or glove."

"I'll get me up before the sun,
I'll cull me boughs off many a tree;
And all alone full early run
To gather flowers and welcome Thee."

"Either disperse these mists, which blot and fill
My perspective still as they pass;
Or else remove me hence unto that hill
Where I shall need no glass!"

"Thy grave, to which my thoughts shall move
Like bees in storms unto their hive."

To arraign Vaughan is to vindicate him. In the too liberal assizes of literature, an idea becomes the property of him who best expresses it. Herbert's odd and fresh metaphors, his homing bees and pricks of conscience and silent tears, the adoring star and the comrade bird, even his famous female scarf, go over bodily to the spoiler. In many an instance something involved and difficult still characterizes Herbert's diction; and it is diverting to watch how the interfering hand sorts and settles it at one touch, and sends it, in Mr. Matthew Arnold's word, to the "centre." Vaughan's mind, despite its mysticism, was full of despatch and impetuosity. Like Herbert, he alludes to himself, more than once, as "fierce"; and the adjective undoubtedly belongs to him. There is in Vaughan, at his height, an imaginative rush and fire which Herbert never knew, a greater clarity and conciseness, a far greater restraint, a keener sense both of color and form, and so much more deference for what Mr. Ruskin calls "the peerage of words," that the younger man could never have been content to send forth a line which might mean its opposite, such as occurs in the fine stanza about glory in the beautiful *Quip*. It is only on middle ground that the better poet and the better saint collide. Vaughan never could have written

"O that I once past changing were
Fast in Thy Paradise, where no flower can wither!"

or the tranquil confession of faith :

"Whether I fly with angels, fall with dust,
Thy hands made both, and I am there:
Thy power and love, my love and trust
Make one place everywhere!"

For his best is not Herbert's best, nor his worst Herbert's worst. It is not Vaughan who reminds us that "filth" lies under a fair face. He does the "fiercer" thing: he goes to the Pit's mouth in a trance, and "hears them yell." Herbert's noblest and most winning art still has its stand upon the altar steps of *The Temple;* but Vaughan is always on the roof, under the stars, like a somnambulist, or actually above and out of sight, "pinnacled dim in the intense inane"; absorbed in larger and wilder things, and stretching the spirits of all who try to follow him. Herbert has had his reward in the world's lasting appreciation; and though Vaughan had a favorable opinion of his own staying powers, nothing would have grieved him less than to step aside, if the choice had lain between him and his exemplar. Or re-risen, he would cry loyally to him, as to that other Herbert, the rector of Llangattock and his old tutor: "*Pars vertat patri, vita posthuma tibi.*"

Vaughan, then, owed something to Herbert, although it was by no means the best which Herbert could give; but he himself is, what Herbert is not, an ancestor. He leans forward to touch Cowper and Keble; and Mr. Churton Collins has taken the pains to trace him in Tennyson.

The angels who

"familiarly confer
Beneath the oak and juniper,"

invoke an instant thought of the Milton

of the *Allegro;* and the fragrant winds which linger by Usk, "loaden with the rich arrear," appear to be Milton's, too. His austere music first sounded in the public ear in 1645, one year before Vaughan, much his junior, began to print. It would seem very unlikely that a Welsh physician should be beholden long after to the manuscripts of the Puritan stripling, close-kept at Cambridge and Horton; but it is interesting to find the prototype of Vaughan's charming lines about Rachel,

"the sheep-keeping Syrian maid,"

in the *Epitaph on the Marchioness of Winchester*, dating from 1631.* Vaughan's dramatic Fleet Street,

"Where the loud whip and coach scolds all the way,"

* Mr. R. H. Stoddard owns a copy of the first edition of *Nieremberg's Meditations*, translated by Vaughan in 1654, and published the following year, which has upon the title-page an autographic "J. M." supposed, by every evidence, to be Milton's. If it be so, the busy Latin Secretary, meditating his grand work, must have been, on his part, a reader and a lover of the man who was almost his equal at golden phrases.

might as well be Swift's, or Crabbe's ; and his salutation to the lark,

> "And now, as fresh and cheerful as the light,
> Thy little heart in early hymns doth sing,"

is like a quotation from some tender sonnet of Bowles, or from his admirer, the young Coleridge who instantly outstepped him. *Olor*, *Silex*, and *Thalia* establish unexpected relationships with genius the most remote from them and from each other. The animated melody of poor Rochester's best songs seems deflected from

> "If I were dead, and in my place,"

addressed to Amoret,* in the *Poems* of 1646. The delicate simile,

> "As some blind dial, when the day is done,
> Can tell us at midnight there was a sun,"

and

> "But I am sadly loose and stray,
> A giddy blast each way.
> O let me not thus range :
> Thou canst not change!"

---

* Congreve and Waller employ the same rather too obvious love-name for their serenaded divinities.

(a verse of a poem headed by an extract, in the Vulgate, from the eighth chapter to the Romans), come home with a smile to the lover of Clough. Vaughan was that dangerous person, an original thinker; and the consequence is that he compromises a great many authors who may never have heard of him. It is admitted now that we owe to his prophetic lyre one of the boasts of modern literature. Dr. Grosart has handled so well the obvious debt of Wordsworth in *The Intimations of Immortality*, and has proven so conclusively that Vaughan figured in the library at Rydal Mount, that little need be said here on that theme. In *Corruption*, *Childhood*, *Looking Back*, and *The Retreat*, most markedly in the first, lie the whole point and pathos of

> "Trailing clouds of glory do we come
> From Heaven, which is our home."

Few studies are more fascinating than that of the liquidation, so to speak, of Vaughan's brief, tense, impassioned monodies into "the mighty waters rolling evermore" of the great *Ode*. It is Holinshed's accidental honor that he is lost in Shakespeare, and incorporated with him. So with Vaughan: if shorn of his dues, he still remains illustrious by virtue of one signal service to Wordsworth, whom, in the main, he distinctly foreshadows. Yet it is no unpardonable heresy to be jealous that the "first sprightly runnings" of a classic should not be better known, and to prefer their touching simplicity to the grandly adult and theory-burdened lines which everybody quotes. In the broad range of English letters we find two persons whose normal mental habits seem altogether of a piece with Vaughan's: a woman of the eighteenth century, and a philosopher of the nineteenth. The lovely *Petition for an Absolute Retreat*, by Anne, Countess of Winchelsea (whose genius was the charming *trouvaille* of Mr. Edmund Gosse), might pass for Vaughan's, in Vaughan's best manner; and so might

"Their near camp my spirit knows
By signs gracious as rainbows,"

as indeed the whole of Emerson's ever-memorable *Forerunners*, itself a mate for

The Retreat; or rather, had these been anonymous lyrics of Vaughan's own day, it would have been impossible to persuade a Caroline critic that he could not name their common author.

Our poet had a curious fashion of coining verbs and adjectives out of nouns, and carried it to such a degree as to challenge pre-eminence with Keats.

> "O how it bloods
> And spirits all my earth!"

is part and parcel of the young cries of Endymion. When Vaughan has discovered something to produce a fresh effect, he is not the man who will hesitate to use it; and this mannerism occurs frequently: "our grass straight russets," "angel'd from that sphere," "the mountained wave," "He heavened their walks, and with his eyes made those wild shades a Paradise." A little informality of this sort sometimes justifies itself, as in the couplet ending the grim and powerful *Charnel-House:*

> "But should wild blood swell to a lawless strain,
> One check from thee shall channel it again!"

And Henry Vaughan shares also with Keats, writing three hundred years later, a defect which he had inherited, together with many graces, directly from Ben Jonson:* the fashion of crowding the sense of his text and the pauseless voice of his reader from the natural breathing-place at the end of a line into the beginning or the middle of the next line. More than any other, except Keats in his first period, he roughens, without always strengthening, his rich decasyllabics, by using what Mr. Gosse has happily classified as the "overflow."

Though the Silurist had in him the possibilities of a great elegiac poet, and his laments for his dead are many and memorable, there is not one sustained masterpiece among them; nothing to equal

* Vaughan openly wears jewels which belong to Jonson.

"Go seek thy peace in war:
Who falls for love of God shall rise a star!"

wrote brave Father Ben; and no Englishman of spirit, between 1642 and the Restoration, was likely to forget it. The passage certainly clung to Vaughan's mind, for he assimilated it later in a sweet line all for peace:

"Do thou the works of day, and rise a star."

or approach, for example, Cowley's *Ode on the Death of Mr. William Hervey*, in the qualities which abide, and are visited with the honors of the class-book and the library shelf. Yet Vaughan's elegies are exquisite and endearing; they haunt one with the conviction that they stop short of immortality, not because their author had too little skill, but because, between his repressed speech and his extreme emotions, no art could make out to live. He had a deep heart, such as deep hearts will always recognize and reverence:

"And thy two wings were grief and love."

In the face of eternity he seems so to accord with the event which all but destroys him, that sorrow inexpressible becomes suddenly unexpressed, and his funeral music ends in a high enthusiasm and serenity open to no misconception. Distance, and the lapse of time, and his own utter reconciliation to the play of events make small difference in his utterance upon the old topic. The thought of his friend, forty years after, is the same mystical rapture:

> "O could I track them! but souls must
> Track one the other;
> And now the spirit, not the dust,
> Must be thy brother:
> Yet I have one pearl by whose light
> All things I see,
> And in the heart of death and night,
> Find Heaven and thee."

Daphnis, the eclogue to the memory of Thomas Vaughan, is the only one of these elegies which, possessing a surplus of beautiful lines, is not even in the least satisfying. "R. Hall," "no woolsack soldier," who was slain at the siege of Pontefract, won from Henry Vaughan a passionate requiem, which opens with a gush of agony, "I knew it would be thus!" as affecting as anything in the early ballads; and the battle of Rowton Heath took from him "R. W.," the comrade of his youth. But it was in one who bore his sovereign's name (hitherto unidentified, although he is said to have been the subject of a "public sorrow") that Vaughan lost the friend upon whom his whole nature seemed to lean. The soldier-heart in himself spoke out firmly in the cry he consecrated *To the Pious Memory of C. W.* Its masculine dignity; the pride and soft triumph which it gathers about it, advancing; the plain heroic ending which sweeps away all images of remoteness and gloom, in

"Good-morrow to dear Charles! for it is day,"

can be compared to nothing but an *agitato* of Schubert's mounting strings, slowing to their major chord with a courage and cheer that bring tears to the eyes. Vaughan's tender threnodies would make a small but precious volume. *To the Pious Memory*, with *Thou that Knowest for Whom I Mourn, Silence and Stealth of Days, Joy of my Life while Left me Here, I Walked the other Day to spend my Hour, The Morning Watch,* and *Beyond the Veil,* are alone enough to give him rank forever as a genius and a good man.

"C. W.'s" death was one of the things which turned him forever from temporal pursuits and pleasures. Of his first wife we can find none but conjectural traces in his books, for he was shy of using the beloved name. The sense of those departed is never far from him. The air of melancholy recollection, not morbid, which hangs over his maturer lyrics, is directly referable to the close-following calamities which estranged him from the presence of "the blessèd few," and sent him, as he nobly hoped,

"Home from their dust to empty his own glass."

His thoughts centred, henceforward, in their full intensity, on the supernatural world; nay, if he were irremediably depressed, not only on the persistence of resolved matter, by means of which buried men come forth again in the color of flowers and the fragrance of the wind, but even on the physical damp and dark which confine our mortality. It is the poet of dawn and of crisp mountain air who can pack horror on horror into his nervous quatrains about Death:

"A nest of nights; a gloomy sphere
 Where shadows thicken, and the cloud
Sits on the sun's brow all the year,
 And nothing moves without a shroud."

This is masterly; but here, again, there is reserve, the curbing hand of a man who holds, with Plato, a wilful indulgence in the "realism" of sadness to be an actual crime. Vaughan's dead dwell, indeed, as his own mind does, in "the world of light." As his corporeal sight is always upon the zenith or the horizon, so his fancy is far away, with his radiant ideals, and with the virtue and beauty he has walked with in the flesh. He takes his harp to the topmost hill, and sits watching

"till the white-winged reapers come."

He thinks of his obscured self, the child he was, and of "the narrow way" (an ever-recurrent Scriptural phrase in his poetry) by which he shall "travel back." To leave the body is merely to start anew and recover strength, and, with it, the inspiring companionship of which he is inscrutably deprived.

Chambers' *Cyclopædia* made an epic blunder, long ago, when it ascribed to this gentlest of Anglicans a "gloomy sectarianism." He, of all religious poets, makes the most charming secular reading, and may well be a favorite with the heathen for whom Herbert is too decorative, Crashaw too hectic and intense, Cowper too fearful, and Faber too fluent; *Lyra Apostolica* a treatise, though a glorious one, on Things which Must be Revived, and *Hymns Ancient and Modern* an exceeding weariness to the spirit. It is a saw of Dr. Johnson's that it is impossible for theology to clothe itself in attractive numbers; but then Dr. Johnson was ignorant of Vaughan. It is not in human nature to refuse to cherish the " holy, happy, healthy Heaven " which he has left us (in a graded alliteration which smacks of the physician rather than of the "gloomy sectarian "), his very social " angels talking to a man," and his bright saints, hovering and smiling nigh, who

> "are indeed our pillar-fires
> Seen as we go ;
> They are the city's shining spires
> We travel to."

Who can resist the earnestness and candor with which, in a few sessions, he wrote down the white passion of the last fifty years of his life? No English poet, unless it be Spenser, has a piety so simple and manly, so colored with mild thought, so free from emotional consciousness. The elect given over to continual polemics do not count Henry Vaughan as one of themselves. His double purpose is to make life pleasant to others and to praise God; and he considers that he is accomplishing it when he pens a compliment to the valley grass, or, like Coleridge, caresses in some affectionate strophes the much-abused little ass. All this liberal sweetness and charity heighten Vaughan's poetic quality, as they deepen the impression of his practical Christianity. The nimbus is about his laic songs. When he talks of moss and rocks, it is as if they were incorporated into the ritual. He has the genius of prayer, and may be recognized by "those graces which walk in a veil and a silence." He is full of distinction, and of a sort of golden idiosyncrasy. Vaughan's true "note" is— Vaughan. To read him is like coming alone to a village church-yard with trees, where the west is dying, in hues of lilac and rose, behind the low ivied Norman tower. The south windows are open, the young choir are within, and the organist, with many a hushed unconventional interlude of his own, is rehearsing with them the psalm of "pleasures for evermore."

III
GEORGE FARQUHAR
1677-1707

GEORGE FARQUHAR

THERE is a narrow dark Essex Street West in the city of Dublin, running between Fishamble Street and Essex Gate, at the rear of the Lower Blind Quay. The older people still bluntly call it what it was called before 1830: Smock Alley. On its north side stands the sufficiently ugly church of SS. Michael and John. The arched passage still in use, parallel with the nave of this church, was the entrance to a theatre on the same site; what is now the burial vault was once the pit, full of ruddy and uproarious faces. The theatre, erected about 1660, which had a long, stormy and eventful history, was rebuilt in 1735, and having been turned into a warehouse, fell into decay, to be replaced by a building of another clay. But while it was still itself, it was great and popular, and the lane between Trinity College and the old arched passage was choked every night with the press of jolly youths, who, as Archbishop King pathetically complained, appeared to love the play better than study! Among those who hung about Smock Alley like a barnacle in the years 1694 and 1695, was a certain George Farquhar, son of William,* a poor Londonderry clergyman of the Establishment; a long-faced peculiar lad of mild mien but high spirits. He had come

* Incipit Annus Academicus Die Julii 9ª 1694.

Die Julii	Georgius Farquhare Sizator	filius Gulielmi Farqhare Clerici	Annos 17	Natus London-derry	ibidem educatus sub magistro Walker	Eu. Lloyd (college tutor)
17a						

This matriculation entry from the register of Trinity does away with our sizar's presumed father, Rev. John Farquhar, prebendary of Raphoe. We hear nothing more, ever after, of the Farquhar family, who henceforth leave young George to his own profane devices; nor can any certainty be attached to additional information, sometimes proffered, that the father had seven children in all, and held a living of only one hundred and fifty pounds a year. One other point is fixed by the entry, to wit: if George Farquhar was seventeen in the July of 1694, he cannot have been born in 1678.

from the north, under episcopal patronage, to wear a queer dress among his social betters, to sweep and scour and carry tankards of ale to the Fellows in hall; and incidentally, to imbibe, on his own part, the lore of all the ages. The major event in his history is that, instead of sitting up nights over *Isocrates de Pace*, he slipped off to see Robert Wilkes and the stock company, and to decide that acting, or, as he afterwards sarcastically defined it, "tearing his Lungs for a Livelihood," was also the thing for him. Wherefore, at eighteen, either because his benefactor, Bishop Wiseman of Dromore, had died, or else, as is not very credibly reported, because he was cashiered from his class, Master Farquhar, cut loose from his old moorings, applied to Manager Ashbury of the Dublin Theatre, and to such avail that he was able presently to make his own appearance there as no less a personage than Othello. He had a weak voice and a shy presence; but the public encouraged him. One of his first parts was that of Guyomar, Montezuma's younger brother, in Dryden's tragedy of *The Indian Emperor*. In the fifth act, as soon as he had declaimed to Vasquez in sounding sing-song:

"Friendship with him whose hand did Odmar kill?
Base as he was, he was my brother still!
But since his blood has washed away his guilt,
Nature asks thine for that which thou hast spilt,"

he made, according to stage directions, a fierce lunge at his too conciliatory foe. Guyomar had armed himself, inadvertently, with a genuine sword, and Vasquez came near enough to being killed in the flesh. The man eventually recovered; but it shows of what impressionable stuff Farquhar was made, that his mental horror and pain, during that moment while he believed he had slain a fellow-creature, should have turned the course of his life. He left the stage; nor would he return to it. Some eight years after, indeed, he visited Dublin again, and on the old boards played Sir Harry Wildair for his own benefit; but this was at a time when he forced himself to undertake all honorable chances of money-making, out of his consuming anxiety for his family.

Wilkes and his wife returned to London, and the lad Farquhar went with them. He obtained a commission in the army from the Earl of Orrery; he was in Holland on duty during a part of the year 1700, and came back to England with one of her earliest military red coats on his back, in the train of his much-approved sovereign, William III. He had already written, thanks to Wilkes and his incessant urging, his first two plays, and had seen them successful at Drury Lane;* he had also overheard with enthusiasm, at the Mitre Tavern in St. James's Market, Mistress Nance Oldfield, an orphan of sixteen, niece of the proprietress, reading *The Scornful Lady* behind the bar. Captain Vanbrugh was duly told of Farquhar's delight and admiration, and on the strength of them introduced the girl to Rich, who did few things so good in his lifetime as when he put her upon the stage at fifteen shillings a week. It was not long before this distinguished actress and generous woman,

* This was the theatre built by Sir Christopher Wren in 1672.

destined to lend her gayety and beautiful bearing to the interpretation of Farquhar's women, enlivened the town as the glorious Sylvia of *The Recruiting Officer*, who can "gallop all the morning after a hunting-horn, and all the evening after a fiddle."

"We hear of Farquhar at one time," says Leigh Hunt, in a pretty summary, "in Essex, hare-hunting (not in the style of a proficient); at another, at Richmond, sick; and at a third, in Shropshire on a recruiting party, where he was treated with great hospitality, and found material for one of the best of his plays."

Love and a Bottle inaugurated the vogue of the Farquhar comedy; and Wilkes, whose name in London carried favor and precedence, was the Roebuck of the cast. Its successors, *The Constant Couple* (with a framework transferred and adapted from its author's earlier *Adventures of Covent Garden*), and its sequel, *Sir Harry Wildair*, again championed by the "friendly and indefatigable" Wilkes, who impersonated the engaging rakish heroes, had long runs, and firmly established their author's fame. In 1702 Farquhar produced *The Inconstant* (which he had perverted from Fletcher's *Wild Goose Chase*, as if a fit setting were sought for the wonderfully effective last act of his own devising); and after *The Inconstant*, *The Twin Rivals*. *The Stage Coach*, a one-act farce in which he had a collaborator,* dates from 1704, and *The Recruiting Officer* from 1706; *The Beaux' Stratagem* was written in the spring of 1707. This is a working record of barely nine years; it represents a secure and continuous artistic advance; and it should have brought its patient originator something better than the privilege of dying young, "broken-hearted," as he confessed to Wilkes, "and without a shilling."

Farquhar had but the trifling income of an officer's pay on which to support his wife and his two little daughters. He seems to have sought no political prefer-

* Peter Anthony Motteux, the wild and clever linguist and dramatist, who made the best English translation of *Don Quixote*. *The Stage Coach*, itself an adaptation, has little merit beyond its liveliness.

ment, nor did his numerous patrons put themselves out to advance him, although these were the very days when men of letters were crowded into the public service. Ever and anon he received fifteen guineas, then a very handsome sum, for a play. Perhaps, like his rash gallants, he had "a head to get money, and a heart to spend it." He greatly wished success, for the sake of those never absent from his thought; and he complained bitterly when the French acrobats and ropedancers took from *The Twin Rivals* the attention of pleasure-seeking Londoners, much as poor Haydon complained afterwards of the crowds who surged down Piccadilly, to behold not his "Christ's Entry into Jerusalem" at all, but General Tom Thumb, holding court under the same roof.

When Farquhar's health was breaking, and debts began to involve him at last, it appears that the Earl of Ormonde, his general, prompted him to sell his commission in order to liquidate them, and agreed to give him a captaincy. Or, as is yet more probable, in view of the fact that Farquhar was already known by the title of captain, he was urged to sell out of the army, on a given pledge that preferment of another sort awaited him. His other industrious devices to secure support for four having missed fire, he gladly performed his part of the transaction, only to experience a fatal delay on the part of my Lord Ormonde, whose mind had strayed to larger matters. In fine, the unkept promise hurt the subaltern to the heart; he sank, literally from that hour, of grief and disquietude. Lintott the stationer, and his old friend Wilkes stood manfully by him, one with liberal payment in advance, and one with affectionate furtherance and gifts; but Farquhar did not rally. It was to Wilkes, as everybody knows, that he penned this most touching testament: "Dear Bob, I have not anything to leave thee to perpetuate my memory but two helpless girls. Look upon them sometimes! and think of him who was, to the last moment of his life, thine." The end came on or about April 29, 1707, George Farquhar being just thirty years of age.

While he lay dying in Soho, his last and best comedy was in progress at the new magnificent Haymarket, and his audiences, with a barren benevolence not uncharacteristic of the unthinking human species, are said to have wept for him. He was buried in the parish church-yard of St. Martin-in-the-Fields,* where Nell Gwynne's contrite ashes lay, and where her legacied bells tolled for his passing.

Farquhar's name is always coupled with those of Congreve, Wycherley, and Vanbrugh, although in spirit and also in point of time he was removed from the influences which formed them. Many critics, notably Hazlitt, Macaulay, and Thackeray, have allowed him least mention of the four, but he is, in reality, the best playwright among them; and it is greatly to the credit of a discreditable

---

* The register of burial is dated a month later than the received date of his death. It reads simply: 23 May, George Falkwere, M." The initial is the sapient sexton's indication that this was neither a W (woman) nor a C (child). The spelling of the name betokens its usual and original pronunciation. The present famous porticoed church was not built for nineteen years after Farquhar died.

period if he be taken as its representative. He had Vanbrugh's exuberant vivacity, Congreve's grace, Wycherley's knack of climax. Wycherley, retiring into private life when Farquhar was born, lived to see his exit; Etherege was then at his zenith; Dryden's *All for Love* was in the printer's case, and Otway, almost on the point of his two great works, was coming home ragged from Flanders: Otway, whose boyish ventures on the stage, and whose subsequent soldiering, Farquhar was so closely to follow.

Pope, and a gentler observer, Steele, found Farquhar's dialogue "low," and so it must have sounded between the brave surviving extravagances of the Jacobean buskin and the modulated utterances of *Cato* and *The Revenge*. A practical talent like Farquhar's was bound to provoke hard little words from the Popes who shrank from his spontaneous style, and the Steeles who could not approve of the gross themes he had inherited. For sheer good-breeding, some scenes in *The Way of the World* can never be surpassed; they prove that one cannot hold the stage by talk alone. It is fortunate for Farquhar that he could not emulate the exquisitely civilized depravities of Congreve's urban Muse. But his dialogue is not "low" to modern tastes; it has, in general, a simple, natural zest, infinitely preferable to the Persian apparatus of the early eighteenth cei..ury. Even he, however, can rant and deviate into rhetoric, as soon as his lovers drop upon one knee. More plainly in Farquhar's work than in that of any contemporary, we mark the glamour of the Caroline literature fading, and the breath of life blowing in. An essentially Protestant nationalism began to settle down upon England for good and all with William and Mary, and it brought subtle changes to bear upon the arts, the trades, the sports, and the manners of the people. In Farquhar's comedies we have the reflex of a dulling and strengthening age; the fantasticalities of the last three reigns are all but gone; the Vandyck dresses gleam and swish no longer. Speech becomes more pert and serviceable, in a vocabulary of lesser range; lives are vulgarizing, that is, humanizing, and getting closer to common unromantic concerns; no such delicately unreal creature as Millamant, all fire and dew and perfumery,— Millamant who could not suffer to have her hair done up in papers written in prose, and who, quite by herself, is a vindication of what Mr. Allibone is pleased to call " Lamb's sophistical and mischievous essay,"—walks the world of Farquhar. With him, notwithstanding that the sorry business to be despatched is the same old amorous intrigue, come in at once less license, less affectation, less Gallicism. He reports from the beginning what he himself apprehends; his plays are shorthand notes, albeit timid in character, upon the transitional and prosaic time. His company is made up of individuals he had seen in a thousand lights at the Spread Eagle and the Rummer; in the Inner Temple and in St. James's Park; in barracks domestic and foreign; and in his native place, where adventurers, eloquent in purest Londonderry,* stum-

* The not altogether foolish censure has been cast upon the rogue Teague in *The Twin Rivals* that he speaks an

bled along full of whiskey and ideas. He anticipates certain phases of Private Ortheris's thorough-going love of London, and figures his exiled Dicky as "just dead of a consumption, till the sweet smoke of Cheapside and the dear perfume of Fleet-ditch" made him a man again. In this laughing affectionate ap-

impossible brogue, which might as well be Welsh. Farquhar did not succeed in transferring to paper the weird and unlovely Ulster dialect with which he was familiar in boyhood, and which had figured already in the third act of *Henry the Fifth*, in Jonson's Irish masque, in Shadwell's *Lancashire Witches;* which was simultaneously being used in his farce *The Committee*, by Dryden's friend Howard, and which was afterwards to have good corroboration in Aytoun's *Massacre of the MacPherson*. Farquhar employs it twice elsewhere, passably well in the case of Torlough Macahone of the parish of Curroughabegley (the personage who built a mansion-house for himself and his predecessors after him), and with lamentable flatness in that of Dugard in his last comedy. Dugard is a rival of the nursery-maid dear to almanac humorists, who is wont to exclaim: "Can't ye tell boi me accint that 'tis Frinch Oi am!" It was one of Farquhar's inartistic mistakes that he made no loving study of this or of anything touching nearly his own people. His Irishmen, with the exception of Roebuck, are either rascals or characterless nobodies. The name Teague, or Teig, which Howard had also employed, is old and pure North Irish; and no less pleasant an authority than George Borrow reminds us in the *Romano Lavo-Lil* that it is Danish in origin.

prehension of the local and the temporal lies Farquhar's whole strength or weakness. From the poets of the Restoration there escapes, most incongruously, now and then, something which betokens a sense of natural beauty, or even a recognition of the divine law; but Farquhar is not a poet, and this spray from the deeps is not in him. He perceives nothing that is not, and opens no crack or chink where the fancy can air itself for a moment and

—"step grandly out into the infinite."

Such a lack would not be worth remarking in the debased and insincere writers who but just preceded him. But from the very date of his first dealings with London managers, idealism was abroad, and a man with affinities for "the things that are more excellent" need have feared no longer to divulge them, since the court and the people, if not the dominant town gentry, were with him. Farquhar had neither the full moral illumination nor the will, though he had the capacity, to lend a hand to the blessed work waiting for the opportunist. He was young, he was of provincial nurture; he was carried away by the theatrical tradition. Yet his mind was a Medea's kettle, out of which everything issued cleaner and more wholesome. Despite the prodigious animal spirits of his characters, they conduct their mad concerns with sense and moderation; they manage tacitly to proclaim themselves as temporarily "on a tear," as going forth to angle in angling weather, and as likely to lead sober citizen lives from to-morrow on. Under bad old maintained conditions they develop traits approximately worthy of the *Christian Hero*. They "look before and after." They are to be classed as neutrals and nondescripts, for they have all the swagger of their lax progenitors, and none of their deviltry. They belong professionally to one family, while they bear a tantalizing resemblance to another. Farquhar himself, perhaps unaware that partisanship is better than compromise, made his bold toss for bays both spiritual and temporal. Imitating, as novices will ever do, the art back of him, he adopted the claim to approbation which that art never dreamed of. In the very good preface to *The Twin Rivals* (which has always been approved of critics rather than of audiences), he sets up for a castigator of vice and folly, and he offers to appease "the ladies and the clergy," as, in some measure apparent to the more metaphysical among them, he may have done. His friend, Mr. John Hopkins, the author of *Amasia*, invited, on behalf of *The Constant Couple*, the commendation of Collier. That openminded censor may have seen with satisfaction, in the general trend of Farquhar's composition, the less and less dubious day-beams of Augustan decency. Though Farquhar did not live, like Vanbrugh and the magnanimous Dryden, to admit the abuse of a gift, and to deplore it, he alone, of the minor dramatists, seems all along to have had a negative sort of conscience better than none. His instincts continually get the better not only of his environment, but of his practice. Some uneasiness, some misgiving, are at the bottom of his homely materialism. He thinks it best, on the whole, to forswear the temptation to be sublime, and to keep to his cakes and ale; and for cakes and ale he had an eminent and inborn talent. What was ably said of Hogarth, the great exemplar, will cover all practicians of his school: "He had an intense feeling for and command over the impressions of senses and habit, of character and passion, the serious and the comic; in a word, of nature as it fell in with his own observation, or came into the sphere of his actual experience. But he had little power beyond that sphere, or sympathy for that which existed only in idea. He was 'conformed to this world, not transformed.'" Or, as Leigh Hunt, in his beautiful memoir, adds, with acuteness, of Farquhar himself: "He could turn what he had experienced in common life to the best account, but he required in all cases the support of ordinary associations, and could not project his spirit beyond them." In short, Farquhar lacked imagination. He had insight, however, of another order, which is his praise, and which distinguishes him from all his fellows: he had sympathy and charity.

The major blot on the literature of the English stage of the period is not its libertinism, but rather its concomitant utter heartlessness. "Arrogance" (so, according to Erasmus, that ascetic scholar Dean Colet used to remind his clergy) "is worse than a hundred concubines." The slight sporadic touches of tenderness, of pity, of disinterested generosity, to be found by patient search in Congreve, come in boldly with Farquhar, and boldly overrun his prompter's books. Vanbrugh's scenes stand on nothing but their biting and extravagant sarcasm. As Congreve's characters are indiscriminately witty, so Vanbrugh's are universally and wearisomely cynical, and at the expense of themselves and all society. His women in high life have no individuality; they wear stings of one pattern. The genial conception of the shrewd, material Mrs. Amlet, however, in *The Confederacy*, is worthy of Farquhar, and certainly Congreve himself could not have bettered her in the execution. Etherege's typical Man of Mode is a tissue of untruth, hardness, and scorn, all in impeccable attire; a most mournful spectacle. Thinking of such dainty monsters, Macaulay let fly his famous invective against their creators: "Foreheads of bronze, hearts like the nether millstone, and tongues set on fire of hell!" George Farquhar may be exempted altogether from this too-deserved compliment. There is honest mirth in his world of fiction, there is dutifulness, there is true love, there are good women; there is genuine friendship between Roebuck and Lovewell, between Trueman and Hermes Wouldbe, between Aimwell and Archer, and between the green Tummas of *The Recruiting Officer* and his Costar, whom he cannot leave behind. Sylvia, Angelica, Constance, Leanthe, Oriana, Dorinda, free-spoken as they are, how they shine, and with what morning freshness, among the tiger-lilies of that evil garden of the Restoration drama! These heroines are an innovation, for they are maids, not wedded wives. As to the immortal periwigged young bloods their suitors, they are "real gentlemen," as Hazlitt, who loved Farquhar, called them, "and only pretended impostors;" or, to quote Farquhar's latest editor, Mr. A. C. Ewald, they are "always men and never yahoos." Their author had no interest in "preferring vice, and rendering virtue dull and despicable." Their praise may be negative, but it establishes a wide wall of difference between them and the fops and cads with whom they have been confounded. In their conversations, glistening with epigram and irony, malevolence has no part; they sneer at no virtue, they tamper with none; and at every turn of a selfish campaign they find opportunity for honorable behavior. From the mouths of these worldlings comes satire, hot and piping, against worldliness; for Farquhar is as moralizing, if not as moral, as he dares be. Some of the least attractive of them, the most greedy and contriving, have moments of sweetly whimsical and optimistic speech. Thus Benjamin Wouldbe, the plotter against his elder brother in *The Twin Rivals*, makes his adieu after the fashion of a true gallant: "I scorn your beggarly benevolence! Had my designs succeeded, I would not have allowed you the weight of a wafer, and therefore will accept none." The same person soars again into a fine Aurelian speculation: "Show me that proud stoic that can bear success and champagne! Philosophy can support us in hard fortune, but who can have patience in prosperity?" Over his men and women in middle life Farquhar lingers with complacence entirely foreign to his colleagues, to whom mothers, guardians, husbands, and other appleguarding dragons were uniformly ridiculous and odious. Justice Balance is as attractive as a hearth-fire on a December night; so is Lady Bountiful. Over Fairbank, the good goldsmith, Farquhar gets fairly sentimental, and permits him to drop unaware into decasyllabics, like the pastoral author of *Lorna Doone*. His rogues are merely roguish, in the softened sense of the word; in his panorama, though black villains come and go, it is only for an instant, and to further some one dramatic effect. He has eulogy for his heroes when they deserve it, and when they do not you may trust him to find a compassionate excuse; as when poor Leanthe feelingly says of her lover that "his follies are weakly founded upon the principles of honor, where the very foundation helps to undermine the structure." Even Squire Sullen, for his lumpishness, is divorced without derision, and in a peal of harmless laughter. Farquhar, indeed, is all gentleness, all kindness. He had the pensive attitude of the true humorist towards the world he laughed at; his characters let slip words too deep for their living auditors. It is curious that to a Restoration dramatist, "a nether millstone," we should owe a perfect brief description of ideal married life. In the scene of the fourth act of *Sir Harry Wildair*, where Lady Lurewell, with her "petrifying affectation," is trying to tease Sir Harry out of all endurance on the subject of his wife (whom he believes to be lost or dead), and the degree of affection he had for her, he makes reply: "My own heart whispered me her desires, 'cause she herself was there; no contention ever rose but the dear strife of who should most oblige—no noise about authority, for neither would stoop to command, where both thought it glory to obey." This is meant to be spoken rapidly, and not without its tantalizing lack of emphasis; but what a pearl it is, set there in the superlatively caustic dialogue! English chivalry and English literature have no such other golden passage in their rubrics, unless it be the famous tribute to the Lady Elizabeth Hastings that "to love her was a liberal education," or Lovelace's unforgettable song:

> "I could not love thee, dear, so much,
> Loved I not Honour more!"

The passage takes on a very great accidental beauty when we remember that it required courage, in its time and place, to have written it. It is characteristic also of Farquhar that it should be introduced, as it is, on the top wave of a vivacious and stormy conversation, which immediately sweeps it under, as if in proof that he understood both his art and his audience. The conjugal tie, among the leaders of fashion, was still something to laugh at and to toy with. Captain Vanbrugh, from whom nobody need expect much edification, had put in the mouth of his Constant, in a play which was a favorite with Garrick, a bit of sense and sincerity quoted, as it deserved to be, by Hunt: " Though marriage be a lottery in which there are a wondrous many blanks, yet there is one inestimable lot in which the only heaven on earth is written." And again: "To be capable of loving one is better than to possess a thousand." This was in 1698, and Farquhar therefore was not first, nor alone, in daring to speak for the derided idea of wedlock. Steele was soon to arise as the very champion of domestic life; and English wit, since he wrote, has never subsisted by its mockery of the conditions which create

"home-keeping days and household reverences."

But it was Farquhar who spoke in behalf of these the most memorable word of his generation. After that lofty evidence of what he must be suspected to have been, it is well to see, as best we may, what manner of man George Farquhar was. And first let us take some extracts from his own account of himself, "candid and modest," as Hunt named it.

He gives us to understand that he had an ardent temperament, held in check by an introspective turn of thought, by natural bashfulness, and by habits of consideration for others. The portrait is drawn from a letter in the *Miscellanies*, of "a mind and person generally dressed in black," and might have come bodily, and with charming grace, from *The Spectator*. "I have very little estate but what lies under the circumference of my hat . . . and should I by misfortune come to lose my head, I should not be worth a groat." "I am seldom troubled by what the world calls airs and caprices, and I think it an idiot's excuse for a foolish action to say: ''Twas my humor.'" "I cannot cheerfully fix to any study which bears not a pleasure in the application." " Long expectation makes the blessing always less to me; I lose the great transport of surprise." " I am a very great epicure; for which reason I hate all pleasure that's purchased by excess of pain. I can't relish the jest that vexes another. In short, if ever I do a wilful injury, it must be a very great one." " I have many acquaintances, very few intimates, but no friend; I mean, in the old romantic way." " I have no secret so weighty but that I can bear it in my own breast." " I would have my passion, if not led, at least waited on by my reason." This last text, repeated elsewhere by Farquhar, which is the counterpart of one in Sir Philip Sidney's *Arcadia*, has interest from the lips of a child of the " dancing, drinking, and unthinking time." Farquhar's face, in the old prints, is wonderfully of a piece with these amiable reports: a handsome, humane, careworn, melancholy young face, the negation of the contemporary idea of the man about town. His constitution, at its best, was but frail. "You are as dear to me," he says, pathetically, to his Penelope, "as my hopes of waking in health to-morrow morning."

A tradition has been received without question by his many critics and biographers, that his chief characters, all cast in the same animated mould, are but incognitos of himself. Highly-colored projections of himself, with latent traits exaggerated, and formed mental restraints removed, they may indeed be. The public, which loves identifications, insisted on finding him revealed in his Archers and Sir Harrys. Whether or not the dramatists of the day had universally the Rembrandtesque whim of painting themselves into their own foregrounds, they were obstinately supposed to do so, with Etherege in Young Bellair, with Otway in Jaffier. But the real Farquhar

—" courteous, facile, sweet,
Hating that solemn vice of greatness, pride,"

with his reserve, his simple dress, his thin, agreeable voice, his early reputation at college for uncongeniality, acting in every emergency whither we can fairly trace him with deliberate high-mindedness, is far enough from the temper of his restless and jocund creations. He wished to remove the impression that he could have been his own model; for he took pains to inscribe *The Inconstant* to his classmate, Richard Tighe, and to compliment him upon his kinship with Mirabel, "a gay, splendid, easy, generous, fine young gentleman"; the applauded type, in short, of all that Farquhar's heroes set out to be. Again, lest he should pass for a realist as rabid as Mademoiselle de Scudéry, who pinioned three hundred and seventy of her acquaintances between the covers of *Clélie*, Farquhar adds this warning to his enthusiastic dedication of *The Recruiting Officer* "to all friends round the Wrekin": "Some little turns of humor that I met with almost within the shade of that famous hill gave the rise to this comedy; and people were apprehensive that, by the example of some others, I would make the town merry at the expense of the country gentleman. But they forgot that I was to write a comedy, not a libel."

He disclaims everywhere, with the same playful decisiveness, the interpretations put upon his designs and actions by the world of overgrown infants which he entertained. Endowed with courage and much personal charm, he had small chance of distinguishing himself upon the field, and for the most part shone at a garrison mess; but he had led a not inadventurous life, in which were incidents of the most pronounced melodrama, with a touch of mystery to enhance their value for the curious. Farquhar had travelled, and with an open, not an insular mind; he had, by his own confession, too deep an acquaintance with wine, and with the nightingales of Spring Gardens, outsinging "the chimes at midnight, Master Shallow"; he had been, in short, though with "melancholy as his every-day apparel," alive and abroad as a private Whig of the Revolution, shy of ladies' notice till it came, and proud of it ever after. When he printed, in his twenty-first year, *The Adventures of Covent Garden*, he added to it a boy's bragging motto: *Et quorum pars magna fui*. The inference seems to have clung closer to him than he found comfortable. He complains, not without significance, in his prose essay upon the drama, that the public think any rôle compounded of " practical rake and speculative gentleman is, ten to one, the author's own character." With the incident which furnished its thrilling closing scenes to *The Inconstant*, Farquhar had probably no connection; he takes pains to state that the hero of it was the Chevalier de Chastillon, quite as if he feared another confusion of himself, as fearless and quick-witted a man, with the "golden swashbucklers" of his imagination. The rumor which confounded them with him has next to nothing to support it. Fortune, fashion, foolhardiness, impudence, were not the stars which shone upon Farquhar's nativity. Such exotic and epic virtues as may flourish under these, such as do adorn the delightful dandies he depicted, surely belonged to him in person; and his quiet habit of living apart and letting the town talk, fixed to perpetuity the belief that he had exploited himself vicariously, for good and all, upon the stage. Certain qualities of his, certain brave truces established with adverse conditions, force one to consider him with more attention and respect than even his brilliant pen invites. It is something to find him diffident and studious in a bacchanalian society, and with such scrupulous sensitiveness that a mere inadvertence in boyhood forbade him ever to fence again;* but his outstanding characteristic, the thing which sets him apart from his brocaded *dramatis personæ*, is his known lasting devotion to the welfare of his family, and his admirable behavior in relation to his early and extraordinary marriage.

In 1702, Farquhar issued a charming and little-known miscellany, called *Love and Business*, " a collection of occasionary verse and epistolary prose." The poetic

---

* Dear Dick Steele, in 1701, while Captain of Fusileers, had a duel thrust upon him; and in parrying, his sword pierced his man. To his remorse may be ascribed his hatred of the custom of duelling, expressed afterwards on every occasion. Steele owed his start in life to James Butler, Duke of Ormonde, who entered him among the boys on the Charterhouse foundation. This peer was grandfather to the man who failed George Farquhar.

exercises are of small importance; but the other data (which survive as a hindrance, rather than as a help, to biographers) come near being of very definite value. All manner of futile guesses have been expended upon the identification of his Penelope. It is given to no mouser to name her with certainty; but, despite the gossip of the greenroom, now as ever too ready to weave romances about the name of George Farquhar, internal evidence is strongly against her having been Anne Oldfield. Yet this is the supposition of most of his editors. Commenting upon one passage touching some villanous stratagem from which Farquhar says he was able to rescue a friend in the Low Countries, a friend with whom he afterwards condoles upon a robbery she had undergone, Leigh Hunt adds that this may have been the woman whom Farquhar subsequently made his wife. A widow, whose Christian name was Margaret, but of whom we know so little else that we cannot say whether she was English, or whether her age considerably exceeded his, conceived a passionate attachment for him, and managed to have it represented to him from several quarters not only that she was kindly disposed towards him, but that it would be well for his opening career if he should seek her hand, as she had estates and revenues. Eventually, after we know not what hesitations natural to a fastidious temperament, he proposed to her and was accepted, and it soon transpired that the bride was quite as penniless as himself. Hunt does not follow out his own hint in the matter of the robbery, though the question, when carefully considered, has a vital import. If the victim were indeed the lady whom Farquhar married later, and if she were indeed robbed, it should signify that she must then have been possessed of some wealth, so that the report given to Farquhar could not have been, up to that time at least, a lie. On the other hand, casuists must decide whether, again in the event of the victim having been correctly identified by Hunt, the robbery itself may not have been an invention meant, after Farquhar had declared his allegiance, to quicken his sympathy, and to soften the coming revelation that the robbery could never have resulted, owing to a defect in the premises! There is very much else about the *Letters* which is confusing and inconsistent. They are so disconnected, and they vary so in tone and manner, as to suggest a doubt whether, if not altogether imaginary, they could have been meant for any one person. A lady is announced as having returned them for publication; she dresses in mourning, and resides now on the Continent, now in London or in the country; her suitor very explicitly states that he had long solicited in vain the honor of her hand; and, in the end, with farewells and an abrupt and unexplained severing, he gives up the quest, with his own admission that he has lost her and that her heart "had no room for him." Now that the recipient of this correspondence, Anne Oldfield or another, should have returned it for commercial purposes, not having been won by the very real passion exhibited in parts of it, seems somewhat peculiar; but to accept as fact that Farquhar himself actually asked these letters back from her, and printed them as they stood, is, under the conditions, absurd, and irreconcilable with our knowledge of his character from other and prior sources. Hunt further suggests that the *Miscellany* was gathered together in some press of pecuniary trouble; and its title, indeed, may hint at a whimsical expectation that Love, being harnessed and sent abroad to arouse curiosity among readers, may return in the way of Business to headquarters. But Farquhar, in his bachelor days, had a fair income, and would not have been so likely to hear the wolf at the door as he was later, when that sound would awake in him a dread not ominous to himself alone. It is possible that the undiscovered register of his marriage bears the date of 1702 or even of 1701; if it were so, that might explain the issue of his only book not in dramatic dress, and the emergency which called it forth. It is difficult indeed to suppose, although modern delicacy in these matters was just then a somewhat unknown quantity, that we have between its covers genuine love-letters hot from the pen. Steele, of an August morning nine years later, inserted in *The Spectator* as the communication of a third person, six of his own notes to his comely and noble *fiancée*, Mary Scurlock. But Farquhar had not Steele's earnestness and love of circumstantial truth, nor his zest for pointing a moral. Or was this publication the sort of thing he would be likely, for a not unworthy purpose, to do? Was he, in reality, a shade more obtuse and misguided than Miss Fanny Brawne? Rather let us believe the *Letters* a work of fiction, and only founded largely upon various bygone moods and incidents of the foregoing two years, which for one reason or another might interest buyers. Such is the description to "dear Sam" of Dryden's erratic funeral, which is almost too keenly rhetorical a summing-up to have been written the next day, or the thoughtful and sensible surveys of the Dutch. The amatory epistles, with their leaven of reality, are presumably edited out of all recognition. They make no defined impression; they do not move forward; they veil impenetrably the traits of the person addressed, who is made to appear as a vanishing unrelenting goddess, deaf and blind to George Farquhar pleading his best. Whatever were the facts, the report of them is chivalrous. Assume for a moment that his wife stands behind the whole of this correspondence, or even behind the latter part of it, and what seemed to constitute a little betrayal in the very worst taste turns out to be an innocent joke. Of course the "lady" (or one of the ladies) lent the manuscripts to the printers; of course Farquhar originated, in order to give color to Mistress Farquhar's known pretence of riches, and their joint subsequent poverty, the magnificent thieving practised upon the never-thieved and the unthievable! One can fancy them both, in their hard chairs in the bare room, laughing well and long, between tears of anxious hope that the more personal element in the *Miscellany* might fetch them from the Covent Garden book-stalls a parcel of fagots and a dinner.

Aside from all theorizing, it is pleasant to know that their life together was a happy one. The consensus of all witnesses, in the significant absence of any contrary voice, affirms that Farquhar, having been trapped, bore himself like the gentleman he was. Two children were born to him, to brighten, but also to sadden, his brief and diligent life. Under his added anxieties he did his royal best; he addressed to their mother, from first to last, no word of reproach for her fraud.

> "The secret pleasure of the generous act
> Is the great mind's great bribe."

In its fragrance of faith and patience and self-sacrificing tenderness, their domestic story can almost rank next after that sacred one of Charles and Mary Lamb.

Farquhar's widow, who had loved him, appears to have loved his memory.* She

* Mrs. Farquhar published in 1711 an octavo volume of the *Plays, Letters, and Verses*. Among the verses figures a poem of six cantos dedicated to the victorious Earl of Peterborough, entitled *Barcelona*. "It was found among my dear deceased husband's writings," says the widow, in her prefatory note. He was not at the siege, and it is possible that the six cantos were a manuscript copy of the effusion of some former comrade. Farquhar was

did not survive her husband many years; for there is reason to suppose she died before 1719, and in penury. Poor Farquhar used to declare that the dread that his family might suffer want was far more bitter to him than death. Wilkes gave at his theatre, in the May of 1708, a benefit for Margaret Farquhar, and twelve years later he was acting as trustee for the young girls Mary and Anne Margaret, whose pension is said by the *Encyclopædia Britannica* to have amounted to thirty pounds; it was obtained through the exertions of Edmund Challoner, to whom their father had dedicated his *Miscellanies*. Wilkes seems to have again aided both the orphans when they came of age. One of them married an humble tradesman, and died early; the other was living in 1764, wholly uneducated, and, as it is said on small authority, as a maid-

---

the author of several songs, one, of highly didactic complexion, having emanated from him at the reputed age of ten. Of these, only two are of fair lyrical quality : the page's song in *Love and a Bottle*, and "Tell me, Aurelia, tell me, pray," which Robert Southey included in his collection.

servant. Farquhar's elder biographers and editors, Ware, Genest, Chetwood, and the rest, writing in this daughter's lifetime, were apparently unconscious of her existence; but the thought of her father's child, old, neglected, and in a menial position, served to anger Leigh Hunt as late as 1842.

Fear and forecast of what is only too likely to befall the helpless, depressed Farquhar in the April long ago, when he lay dying of consumption, and when, with a fortitude which sustained him under his bitter disappointment, for six weeks, he wrote and finished his masterly comedy *The Beaux' Stratagem*. As he drew near the end of the second act he was told to give up hope; but the second act closes with the famous rattling catechism between Cherry and Archer, and the best bit of verse its author ever made; and the third starts in with the hearty sweet laugh — Anne Oldfield's laugh—of that "exquisite creature, Mrs. Sullen." On a fund of grief, Farquhar enriched his London with a legacy of perpetual merriment. The unflagging impetus of his dramas, above and beyond their very real intrinsic merit, accounts for their great and yet unforfeited popularity. They descend to us associated with the intellectual triumphs of the most dear and dazzling names upon the English stage; they move upon the wings of intelligence and good-nature; they "give delight, and hurt not." They swarm with soldiers, welcome figures long tacitly prohibited from the boards, as too painful a reminder of the Civil Wars. They begin with the clatter of spurs, the bang of doors, the hubbub of bantering voices in "a broadside of damme's." Sergeant Kite appears, followed by a mob on whom he lavishes his wheedling, inspiriting gibble-gabble; Roebuck enters in fantastic colloquy with a beggar; Sir Harry crosses the road, singing, with footmen after him, and Vizard meanwhile indicating him to Standard as "the joy of the playhouse and the life of the park, Sir Harry Wildair, newly come from Paris"; *The Twin Rivals* opens in a volley of epigrams; the rise of the curtain in *The Beaux'*

Stratagem discloses sly old Boniface and the ingenious Cherry calling and running, running and calling, in a fluster pregnant of farce and revel. Farquhar's pages are not for the closet; they have little passive charm; to quote from them, full as they are of familiar saws almost all his own, is hardly fair. His mother-wit arises from the ludicrous and unforeseen predicament, not from vanity and conscious power; it is integral, not mere repartee; and it never calls a halt to the action. As was well said by Charles Cowden Clarke, "there are no traps for jests" in Farquhar; "no trains laid to fire *équivoque*." The clear fun, spurting unannounced in dialogue after dialogue, in incident after incident; the incessant Molière-like masquerades; the thousand little issues depending upon by-play and transient inspiration; the narrowing scope and deepening sentiment of the plot, like a secret given to the players, to be told fully only to the audience most in touch with them—these commend Farquhar's vivacious rôles to actors, and make them both difficult and desirable. With what unction, from an actor's lips, falls his manifold and glowing praise of theatres! What a pretty picture, a broad wash of rose-purple and white, he can make of the interior seen from the wings! "There's such a hurry of pleasure to transport us; the bustle, noise, gallantry, equipage, garters, feathers, wigs, bows, smiles, ogles, love, music, and applause!" And again, in another mood: "The playhouse is the element of poetry, because the region of beauty; the ladies, methinks, have a more inspiring, triumphant air in the boxes than anywhere else. They sit commanding on their thrones, with all their subject slaves about them; their best clothes, best looks; shining jewels, sparkling eyes; the treasures of the world in a ring." And Mirabel, who is speaking, ends with an ecstatic sigh: "I could wish that my whole life long were the first night of a new play!"

This is a drop, or a rise, from Congreve and his aristocratic abstractions. Farquhar, in his youth, had modelled himself chiefly upon the comedy of Congreve, and may be said to have perfected the mechanism which the genius of Congreve had brought into vogue. He never attained, nor could attain, Congreve's scholarly elegance of proportion and his consummate diction. But he had the happiness of being no purely literary dramatist; he had technical knowledge and skill. He brought the existing heroes with their conniving valets, the buxom equivocal maids, the laughing, masking, conscienceless fine ladies, out of their disreputable moonlight into healthful comic air; and added to them, in the transfer, a leaven of homely lovableness which will forever keep his masterpieces upon the stage.

Farquhar's original intellect has a value only relative; he may be considered as Goldsmith's tutor rather than as Congreve's disciple. Goldsmith had no small knowledge of Farquhar, his forerunner by sixty years as a sizar student of Trinity; and, like him, he is reported to have been dropped from his class for a buffoonery. What friends (*Arcades ambo*, in both Virgilian and blameless Byronese) might .

these two parsons' sons have been! Scrub, Squire Sullen's servant, in *The Beaux' Stratagem*, who "on Saturday draws warrants, and on Sunday draws beer," was a part Goldy once greatly desired to act. He, too, when he came to write plays, cast about for conventional types to handle and improve. Tony and his incomparable mother would hardly have been, without their first imperfect apparition in Wycherley's powerful (and stolen) *Plain Dealer;* and Young Marlow and Hastings are frank reproductions of Archer and Aimwell, in a much finer situation. Miss Hardcastle hopes that in her cap and apron she may resemble Cherry. And no one seems to have traced a celebrated passage in *The Vicar of Wakefield* either to my Lady Howdye's message to my Lady Allnight repeated by Archer (who in this same scene introduces the "topical song" upon the modern boards), or else to the example of the manœuvring Bisarre in Act II., Scene I., of *The Inconstant*. Surely, "forms which proceed from simple enumeration and are exposed to validity from a contradictory instance" supplies the unique original of the nonsense-rhetoric which so confounded poor Moses.* The talk of Clincher Junior and Tim, of Kite, Bullock, Scrub, Lyric, and the unbaptized wench Parly, of the constable showing the big bed to Hermes Wouldbe, the talk; that is, of Farquhar's common people, shows humor altogether of what we may call the Goldsmith order: genial, odd, grotesque paradox, springing from Irish inconsequence and love of human kind.

In the sixth year of Queen Anne, when Farquhar died, Steele was married to his "Prue," and having seen the last of his three reformatory dramas "damned for its piety," sought Joseph Addison's approval and collaboration, and fell to designing *The Tatler*. Fielding was newborn, Johnson just out of the cradle,

---

* *The Vicar of Wakefield* dates from 1766. Almost twenty years before that, the immortal Partridge had remarked to Tom Jones, quoting his schoolmaster: " Polly matete cry town is my daskalon." Noble nonsense hath her pedigree. Goldsmith, however, is not so likely to have taken his cue from Fielding.

Pope was trying a cunning young hand at his first *Pastorals;* Defoe, an alumnus of Newgate, was beating his way outward and upward; Swift, yet a Whig, was known but for his *Tale of a Tub*. The fresh waters were rising on all sides to vivify the sick lowlands of the decadence. The kingdoms had a forgotten lesson, and long in the learning, set before them: to regain, as a basis for legitimate results, their mental independence and simplicity; to serve art for art's sake, and to achieve, through the reactionary formalism of the nascent eighteenth century, freedom and a broad ethic outlook. It was as if Comedy, in her winning meretricious perfections, had to die, that English prose might live. It is enough for an immature genius of the third order, born under Charles the Second, to have vaguely foreshadowed a just and imperative change. Farquhar certainly does foreshadow it, albeit with what theologians might call absence of the necessary intention.

He wrote excellent prefaces and prologues. His *Discourse upon Comedy*, in the *Miscellanies*, did pioneer work for his theory, since expounded by more authoritative critics, and received by the English world, that the observance or non-observance of the dramatic unities is at the will of the wise, and that for guidance in all such matters playwrights should look to Shakespeare rather than to Aristotle. The *Discourse*, in Farquhar's clear, sunny, homespun, forceful style, does him honor, and should be reprinted. His best charm is that he cannot be didactic. His suasion is of the strongest, but he has the self-consciousness of all sensitive and analytic minds, which keeps him free here as elsewhere from the slightest assumption of despotism. It is very refreshing, in the face of that incessant belaboring of the reader which Lesage was setting as a contemporaneous fashion, to come across Farquhar's gentle good-humored salutatory : " If you like the author's book, you have all the sense he thought you had ; if you dislike it, you have more sense than he was aware of!" Had he lived longer, or a little later, we should have found him as well, with his turn for skirmishing psychology, among the essayists and the novelists. There were in him a mellowness and an unction which have their fullest play in professedly subjective writing. Farquhar, after all, did not fulfil himself, for he followed an ill outgoing fashion in æsthetics rather than further a right incoming one. No one can help begrudging him to the period he adorned. He deserved to flourish on the manlier morrow, and to hold a historic position with the regenerators of public taste in England. "Ah, go hang thyself up, my brave Crillon, for at Arques we had a fight, and thou wert NOT in it!" One can fancy Sir Richard Steele forever quoting that at Captain George Farquhar, in some roomy club-window in Paradise.

IV
TOPHAM BEAUCLERK
1739–1780
AND
BENNET LANGTON
1741–1800

TOPHAM BEAUCLERK AND BENNET LANGTON

ON Samuel Johnson's famous circle nearly every man stands for himself, full of definite purpose and power. But two young men are there who did nothing of moment, whose names chime often down the pages of all his biographies, and to whom the world must pay honor, if only for the friendship they took and gave. As Apollo should be set about with his Graces "tripping neatly," so the portentous old apparition of Johnson seems never so complete and endearing as when attended by these two above all things else Johnsonians. When the Turk's Head is ajar in Gerrard Street, in shadow-London; when the "unclubable" Hawkins strides over the threshold, and Hogarth goes by the window with his large nod and smile; when Chamier is there reading, Goldsmith posing in purple silk small-clothes, Sir Joshua fingering his trumpet, Burke and little brisk Garrick stirring "bishop"* in their glasses, and the king of the hour, distinguished by his lack of ruffles, is rolling about in his chair of state, saying something prodigiously humorous and wise, it is still Bennet Langton and Topham Beauclerk who most give the scene its human genial lustre, standing with laughter behind him, arm in arm. They were his favorites, and it is the most adorable thing about them both that they made out to like James Boswell, who was jealous of them. (Perhaps they had apprehended thoroughly Newman's fine aphorism concerning a bore: "You may yield, or you may flee: you cannot conquer!") The rare glimpses we have of their brotherly lives is through the door which opens or shuts for Johnson. Between him and them was deep and enduring affection,

---

* A popular eighteenth-century beverage, composed of wine, orange, and sugar.

and what little is known of them has a right to be more, for his sake.

Bennet Langton, born in 1741 in the very neighborhood famous now as the birthplace of Tennyson, was the elder son of the odd and long-descended George Langton of Langton, and of Diana his wife, daughter of Edmund Turnor, Esquire, of Stoke Rochford, Lincolnshire. While a lad in the fen-country, he read *The Rambler*, and conceived the purest enthusiasm for its author. He came to London, indeed, on the ideal errand of seeking him out, and, thanks to the kind apothecary Levett, found the idol of his imagination at home at No. 17 Gough Square, Fleet Street. Despite the somewhat staggering circumstances of Johnson's attire,— for the serious boy had rashly presupposed a stately, fastidious, and well-mannered figure,— he paid his vows, and commended himself to his new friend for once and all. Langton entered Trinity College, Oxford, in 1757, at the age of sixteen.* The Doctor, who

---

* Although Langton is recorded on his college books as having given the usual £10 for plate, and also as

had known him about three years, followed his career at the university with interest, writing to Langton's tutor, then "dear Tom Warton," just appointed to the professorship of poetry held by his father, and afterwards poet-laureate: "I see your pupil: his mind is as exalted as his stature," and to Langton's self the sweet generality: "I love, dear sir, to think of you." He even paid his Freshman a visit, and swam sportively across a dangerous pool in the Isis, in the teeth of his warning; and here also, in the Oxford which was long ago his own "tent of a night," he fell across a part of his destiny in the shape of that strange bird, Mr. Topham Beauclerk, then a taking scapegrace of eighteen. The Doctor must have shaken his head at first, and wondered at the juxtaposition of this arrant Lord of Misrule and the "evan-

---

having paid his caution money in 1757, his name is not down upon the matriculation lists, possibly because he failed to appear at the moment the entries were being made. In what must have been his destined space upon one of the pages, Dr. Ingram made this note: "Q. Num Bennet Langton hic inserendus?"

gelical goodness" of his admirable Langton, until mollified by the knowledge that a species of cult for himself, and ardent perusal of his writings, had first brought them together. It was a pleasant thought to him, that of the two young ribboned heads high in the quadrangle, bending for the ninth time over *The Reasons Why Advice is Generally Ineffectual*, *The Mischief of Unbounded Raillery*, and the jolly satire on *Screech-Owls;* or smiling over the shy Verecundulus and the too-celebrated Misellus who were part of the author's machinery for adding "Christian ardor to virtue, and Christian confidence to truth."

Beauclerk, like Langton, was a critic and a student; he was well-bred, urbane, and of excellent natural parts; moreover, he was a wit, one of the very foremost of his day, when wits grew in every garden. An only child, he was born in London in the December of 1739, and named after that benevolent Topham of Windsor who left the manors of Clewer Brocas and Didworth and a collection of paintings and drawings to his father, the handsome wild Lord Sydney Beauclerk, fifth son of the first Duke of St. Albans, and also, in his time, a gentleman commoner of Trinity. Lord Sydney died early, in the autumn of 1744, and was buried in Westminster Abbey with his hero-brother Aubrey, whose epitaph, still to be read there, Thomson seems to have written. All the pretty toys and curios passed to Topham the little boy, under the guardianship of Lady Beauclerk, his excellent but literal mother, once Mary Norris of Speke in Lancashire. His tutor was named Parker, and must have been a much-enduring man. Young Beauclerk grew up, bearing a resemblance in many ways to Charles II.; and so it befell that with his aggravating flippancy, his sharp sense, his quiver full of gibes, his time-wasting, money-wasting moods, foreign as Satan and his pomps to those of his sweet-natured college companion, he was able to strike Dr. Johnson in his own political weak spot. A flash of the liquid Stuart eye was enough to disarm Johnson at the very moment when he was calling up his most austere frown;

it was enough to turn the vinegar of his wrath to the honey of kindness. *Il ne nous reste qu'une chose à faire : embrassons-nous!* as the wheedling Prince, at a crisis, says to Henry Esmond. Johnson, as everybody knows, was a Jacobite. No sincerer testimony could he have given to his inexplicable liking for a royal rogue than that he allowed Nell Gwynn's great-grandson to tease him and tyrannize over him during an entire lifetime. A choice spectacle this : Mr. Topham Beauclerk, on his introduction, literally bewitching Dr. Samuel Johnson! The stolid moralist was enraptured with his Jack-o'-lantern antics; he rejoiced in his manners, his taste and literary learning; admired him indiscreetly, rich clothes, equipage, and all; followed his whims meekly, expostulated with him almost against his traitorous impulses, and clung to him to the end in unbroken fondness and faith.

Beauclerk had immense gayety and grace, and the full force given by high spirits. His accurate, ever-widening knowledge of books and men, his consummate culture, and his fearlessness, sat handsomely on one who was regarded by contemporary old ladies as a mere " macaroni." It was a matter of course that he tried for no degree at college. The mistress of Streatham Park, who was by no means his adorer, and who remembered his chief wickedness in remembering that " he wished to be accounted wicked," informs us in a private jotting since published that he was "a man of very strict veracity." A philosopher and a truth-teller, whatever his worldly weaknesses, was sure to be a character within the range of Johnson's affections. It was he who most troubled the good Doctor, he for whom he suffered in silence, with whom he wrangled; he whose insuperable taunting promise, never reaching any special development, vexed and disheartened him; yet, perhaps because of these very things, though Bennet Langton was infinitely more to his mind, it was Absalom, once again, whom the old fatherly heart loved best. Nor was he unrepaid. None loved him better, in return, than his " Beau," the very mirror of the name, who was wont to pick his way up the grimy Fleet Street courts "with veneration," as Boswell records.

Bennet Langton, as Mr. Forster expresses it in his noble *Life of Goldsmith*, was "an eminent example of the high and humane class who are content to 'ring the bell' to their friends." He was a mild young visionary, scrupulous, tolerant, and generous in the extreme; modest, contemplative, averse to dissipation; a perfect talker and reader, and a perfect listener; with a face sweet as a child's, fading but now, among his kindred, on the canvas of Sir Joshua Reynolds. He left a gracious memory behind at Oxford, where his musing bust adorns the old monastic library of Trinity. He was six feet six inches tall, slenderly built, and slightly stooping. "The ladies got about him in drawing-rooms," said Edmund Burke, "like maids about the Maypole!"

Miss Hawkins, in her *Memoirs*, names him as the person with whom Johnson was certainly seen to the fairest advantage. His deferent suave manner was the best foil possible to the Doctor's extraordinary explosions. He had supreme self-command; no one ever saw him angry; and in most matters of life, as a genuine contrast to his beloved friend Beauclerk, he was apt to take things a shade too seriously. We learn from Mr. Henry Best, author of some good *Personal and Literary Memorials*, that the advance rumors of the French Revolution found Langton, in the fullest sense, an aristocrat; but it was not long before he became, from conviction, a thorough Liberal, and so remained, although he suffered a great unpopularity, owing to this change, in his native county. He wrote, in 1760, a little book of essays entitled *Rustics*, which never got beyond the passivity of manuscript. The year before, under the date of July 28th, Langton contributed to the pages of *The Idler* the paper numbered 67 and entitled *A Scholar's Journal*. It is a pleasant study of procrastination and of shifting plans, a gentle bit of humor to be ranked as autobiographic. There is an indorsement of Montrose in its heroic advice to "risk the certainty of little for the chance of much." But Langton's graceful academic pen was not destined to a public career. Perseverance of any sort was not native to him. He fulfilled beautifully, adds the vivacious Miss Hawkins, "the pious injunction of Sir Thomas Browne, 'to sit quietly in the soft showers of Providence,' and might, without injustice, be characterized as utterly unfit for every species of activity." Yet at the call of duty, so well was the natural man dominated by his unclouded will, he girded himself to any exertion. Wine-drinking was habitual with him, and he felt its need to sharpen and rouse his intellect; "but the idea of Bennet Langton being what is called 'overtaken,'" wrote the same associate whom we have been quoting, "is too preposterous to be dwelt on." She furnishes one illustration of Langton's Greek serenity. Talking to a company, of a chilly forenoon, in his own house, he paused to remark that if the fire lacked attention it might go out: a brief, casual, murmurous interruption. He resumed his discourse, breaking off presently, and pleading abstractedly with eye in air: "Pray ring for coals!" All sat looking at the fire, and so little solicitous about the impending catastrophe that presently Langton was off again on the stream of his softened eloquence. In a few minutes came another lull. " Did anybody answer that bell?" A general negative. " Did anybody ring that bell?" A sly shaking of heads. And once more the inspired monody soared among the clouds, at last dropping meditatively to the hearthstone: " Dear, dear, the fire is out!"

Langton was the centre of a group, wherever he happened to be, talking delightfully, and twirling the oblong goldmounted snuff-box, which promptly appeared as sociabilities began: a conspicuous figure, with his height, his courteous smile, his mild beauty, and his habit of crossing his arms over his breast, or locking his hands together on his knee. He was a great rider, and could run like a hound. He had a queerness of constitution which seemed to leave him at his lowest ebb every afternoon about two of the clock, forgetful, weary, confused, and without an idea in his head;

but after a little food, he was himself again. At dinner-parties he usually rose fasting, "such was the perpetual flow of his conversation, and such the incessant claim made upon him." A morning call from Mr. Langton was a thing to suggest the eternal years; yet we are told that satiety dwelt not where he was; like Cowley, "he never oppressed any man's parts, or put any man out of countenance." He had much the same sense of humor as Beauclerk had, and his speech was quite as full of good sense and direct observation, if not as cutting. He indicted a fault of Edmund Burke's in one extreme stroke: "Burke whisks the end of his tail in the face of an arguer!" Johnson, the arch-whisker of tails, was not to be brought to book; but Burke's greatness was of a texture to bear and enjoy the thrust. It is curious that Langton was markedly fond of *Hudibras;* such a relish indicates, perhaps, the turn his own wit might have taken, had it not been held in by too much second thought.

Johnson was wont to announce that he

valued Langton for his piety, his ancient descent, his amiable behavior, and his mastery of Greek. "Who in this town knows anything of Clenardus, sir, but you and I?" he would say. In the midst of his talk Langton would fall into the "vowelled undertone" of the tongue he loved, correcting himself with a little wave of the hands, and the apologetic phrase: "And so it goes on." "Steeped to the lips in Greek" he was indeed, bursting out with a joyous salute to the moon of Hellas, upon a friend's doorstep, or making grotesque Hellene puns, for his own delight,* upon the blank leaves of a pocket-book. Every one familiar with Johnsoniana will recall the charming and spirited retort written by Dr. Barnard, then Dean of Derry, later, Bishop of Killaloe, which closes:

> "If I have thoughts and can't express 'em,
> Gibbon shall teach me how to dress 'em
>   In terms select and terse;
> Jones teach me modesty and Greek;
> Smith, how to think; Burke, how to speak;
>   And Beauclerk, to converse!"

* A boyish fashion of self-entertainment afterwards in great favor with Shelley.

In all deference to the illustrious Sir William Jones, it may be claimed that "modesty and Greek" were the very arts in which Langton was a past-master. But he was an amateur, and a private scholar, and his name was a dissyllable; else the Dean might have tossed at his feet as pretty a compliment as that given in the last line to his colleague. It must have gratified Johnson that Langton refused, at Reynolds's dinner-table, "like a sturdy scholar," to sign the famous Round Robin (not signed, either, by Beauclerk) which besought him to "disgrace the walls of Westminster with an English inscription." And as if to keep Langton firmly of his own mind on the subject, it was to him the Doctor confided the Greek quatrain, sad and proud, which he had dedicated to Goldsmith's* memory.

For Bennet Langton Johnson had no

* It is a pleasant thing to remember that it was Langton, always an appreciator of Goldsmith's lovable genius, who suggested "Auburn" as the name for his *Deserted Village*. There is a hamlet called Auborne in Lincolnshire.

criticism but praise. He presented him with pride to Young and to Richardson, described him handsomely to Hannah More, and proceeded to draw his character for Miss Reynolds, ere she had met him, with such "energy and fond delight" as she avowed she never could forget. What fine ringing metal was Johnson's commendation! "He is one of those to whom Nature has not spread her volumes, nor uttered her voices, in vain." "Earth does not bear a worthier gentleman." "I know not who will go to Heaven if Langton does not." And in the sweetest and completest approval ever put by one mortal upon another: "*Sit anima mea cum Langtono!*" Yet even with this "angel of a man" the Doctor had one serious and ludicrous quarrel.

It was the fatal outcome of his uneven moods that he must needs be disenchanted at times even with his best beadsmen: there came days when he would deny Beauclerk's good-humor to be anything but "acid," Langton's anything but "muddy." He considered it the sole grave fault of the latter that he was too ready to introduce a religious discussion into a mixed assembly, where he knew scarcely any two of the company would be of the same mind. On Boswell's suggestion that this may have been done for the sake of instructing himself, Johnson replied angrily that a man had no more right to take that means of gaining information than he had to pit two persons against each other in a duel for the sake of learning the art of self-defence. Some indiscretion of this sort on Langton's part seems to have alienated the friends for the first and last time. It was during their transient bitterness that the Doctor made the historic apology, across the table, to Oliver Goldsmith; an incident which, however beautiful in itself, was a hard back-handed hit at Langton, standing by. Croker's conjecture may be true that the business which threatened to break a fealty of some sixteen years' standing arose rather from Langton's settling his estate by will upon his sisters, whose tutor he had been. On hearing of it, the Great Cham grumbled and fumed, politely applying to the Misses Langton the title of "three dowdies!"* and shouting, in a feudal warmth, that "an ancient estate, sir! an ancient estate should always go to males." In fact, the Doctor behaved very badly, very sardonically, and was pleased to lay hold of a post by Temple Bar one night, and roar aloud over a piece of possible folly up in Lincolnshire which concerned him not in the least. But in due time the breach, whatever its cause, was healed. The Doctor, in writing of it, uses one of his balancing sentences: "Langton is a worthy fellow, without malice, though not without resentment." The two could not keep apart very long, despite all the unreason in the world. "Johnson's quarrels," Mr. Forster tells us, "were lovers' quarrels." Another memorable passage-at-arms, rich in comedy, happened in the course of one of Johnson's sicknesses, when, in

---

* Langton's sisters are generally spoken of as three in number. But Burke's *History of the Landed Gentry* mentions but two, Diana and Juliet. There was a younger brother, Ferne, who died in boyhood, and the floral name, not unlike a girl's, may have been responsible for the confusion.

the cloistral silence of his chamber, he solemnly implored Bennet Langton, always the companion who comforted his sunless hours, to tell him wherein his life had been faulty. His shy and sagacious monitor wrote down, as accusation enough, various Scriptural texts recommending tolerance, humility, long-suffering, and other meek ingredients which were not predominant in the sinner's social composition. The penitent earnestly thanked Langton on taking the paper from his hand, but presently turned his short-sighted eyes upon him from the pillow, and emerging from what his own verbology would call a "frigorific torpor," he exclaimed in a loud, wrathful, suspicious tone: "What's your drift, sir?" "And when I questioned him," so Johnson afterwards told his blustering tale— "when I questioned him as to what occasion I had given him for such animadversion, all that he could say amounted to this: that I sometimes contradicted people in conversation! Now, what harm does it do any man to be contradicted?" To this same paternal young

Langton the rebel submitted his Latin verses; the *Poemata*, in the shape in which we possess them, were rigorously edited by him. And Johnson leaned upon him in more intimate ways, as he could never lean upon Beauclerk. To the scrupulous nature instinctively right he made comfortable confidences: "Men of harder minds than ours will do many things from which you and I would shrink; yet, sir, they will, perhaps, do more good in life than we."

As to the Honorable Topham Beauclerk, more volatile than Langton, he had as steady a "sunshine of cheerfulness" for his heritage. We find him complaining to a friend in the July of 1773: "Every hour adds to my misanthropy; and I have had a pretty considerable share of it for some years past." This incursion of low spirits was not normal with him. Johnson, bewailing his own morbid habits of mind, once said: "Some men, and very thinking men, too, have not these vexing thoughts. Sir Joshua Reynolds is the same all the year round; Beauclerk, when not ill and in pain, is the same." Boswell attests that Beauclerk took more liberties with Johnson than durst any man alive, and that Johnson was more disposed to envy Beauclerk's talents than those of any one he had ever known. Born into the freedom of London, Beauclerk was familiar with Fox, Selwyn, and Walpole, and with the St. James men who did not ache to consort with Johnson; and he was quite their match in ease and astuteness. He walked the modish world, where Langton could not and would not follow; he alternated the Ship Tavern and the gaming-table with the court levees; Davies's shop with the golden insipidities of the drawing-room; *la comédie, la danse, l'amour même,* with the intellectual tie-wigs of Soho. It shows something of his spirit that whereas no member of the Club save himself was a frequenter of White's and Betty's,* or a chosen guest at Strawberry Hill, yet there was no person of fashion whom he was not proud to make known to Doctor Johnson, whenever he judged

* The fruiterer.

the candidate for so genuine an honor worthy of it. Some of these encounters must have been queer and memorable!

Beauclerk's unresting sarcasm often flattened out Boswell and irritated the Doctor, though Bennet Langton, in his abandonments of enthusiastic optimism, was never more than grazed. It is not to be denied that this spoiled child of the Club liked to worry Goldsmith, the maladroit great man who might have quoted often on such occasions the sad gibe of Hamlet:

> "I'll be your foil, Laertes: in mine ignorance
> Your skill shall, like a star in the darkest night,
> Stick fiery off indeed."

What a pity that Goldsmith's *Retaliation* was never finished, so as to include his portrait of Beau! He was "a pestilent wit," as Anthony à Wood calls Marvell. Johnson, shy creature! deplored Beauclerk's "predominance over his company." The tyranny, however, was gracefully and decorously exercised, if we are to believe the unique eulogy that "no man was ever freer, when he was about to say a good thing, from a look which expressed that it was coming; nor, when he had said it, from a look which expressed that it had come." Few human beings have had a finer sense of fun than Topham Beauclerk. He had an infallible eye for the values of blunders, and an incongruity came home to him like a blessing from above. Life with him was a night-watch for diverting objects and ideas. When he was not studying, he was disporting himself, like the wits of the Restoration; and he was equal to all emergencies, as they succeeded one another. Every specimen preserved of his talk is perfect of its kind, and makes us long for a full index. Pointed his speech was, always, and reminds one indeed of a foil, but without the button; a dangerous little weapon, somewhat unfair, but carried with such consummate flourish that those whom it pricks could almost cheer it. "O Lord! how I did hate that horrid Beauclerk!" Mrs. Piozzi scribbled once on the margin of Wraxall's *Memoirs*, in an exquisite feminine vindication of poor Beau's accomplished tongue.

He was no disguiser of his own likes and dislikes. Politics he avoided as much as possible; but he affected less concern in public matters than he really felt. "Consecrate that time to your friends," he writes with mock severity to the ideal Irishman, Lord Charlemont, "which you spend in endeavoring to promote the interests of a half-million of scoundrels." For his private business he had least zeal of all; and cites "my own confounded affairs" as the cause of his going into Lancashire. Beauclerk had great tact, boldness, and independence; his natural scorn of an oppressor was his modern and democratic quality. His idleness (for he was as idle by habit as Langton was by nature) he recognized, and lightly deprecated. Fastidious in everything, he made "one hour of conversation at Elmsley's"* his standard of enjoyment, and his imagined extreme of annoyance was "to be clapped on the

* The bookseller's.

back by Tom Davies." What he chose to call his leisure (again the ancestral Stuart trait!) he dedicated to the natural sciences in his beloved laboratory. " I see Mr. Beauclerk often, both in town and country," wrote Goldsmith to Bennet Langton; "he is now going directly forward to become a second Boyle, deep in chemistry and physics." When there was some fanciful talk of setting up the Club as a college, "to draw a wonderful concourse of students," Beauclerk, by unanimous vote, was elected to the professorship of Natural Philosophy.

Johnson's influence on him, potent though it was, seems to have been negative enough. It kept him from a few questionable things, and preserved in him an outward decorum towards customs and established institutions; but it failed to incite him to make of his manifold talents the "illustrious figure" which Langton's eyes discerned in a vain anticipation. Beauclerk and the great High Churchman went about much together, and had amusing experiences. On such occasions, as in all their familiar intercourse, the disciple had the true salt of the Doctor's talk, which, as Hazlitt remarks, was often something quite unlike "the cumbrous cargo of words" he kept for professional use. In the late winter of 1765 the two visited Cambridge, Beauclerk having a mind to call upon a friend at Trinity.

These, as we know, had their many differences, "like a Spanish great galleon, and an English man-o'-war"; the one smooth, sharp, and civil, the other indignantly dealing with the butt-end of personality. Boswell gives a long account of a charming dispute concerning the murderer of Miss Reay, and the evidence of his having carried two pistols. Beauclerk was right; but Johnson, with quite as solid a sense of virtue, was angry; and he was soothed at the end only by an adroit and affectionate reply. "Sir," the Doctor began, sternly, at another time, after listening to some mischievous waggery, "you never open your mouth but with the intention to give pain, and you often give me pain, not from the power of what you say, but from seeing your intention." And again, he said to him whom he had compared to Alexander, marching in triumph into Babylon: "You have, sir! a love of folly, and a scorn of fools; everything you do attests the one, and everything you say the other."* Beauclerk could also lecture his mentor. It was his steadfast counsel that the Doctor should devote himself to poetry, and draw in his horns of dogma and didactics.

He had, ever ready, some quaint simile or odd application from the classics; in the habit of "talking from books," as the Doctor called it, he was, however, distanced by Langton. Referring to that friend's habit of sitting or standing against the fireplace, with one long leg twisted about the other, "as if fearing to occupy too much space," Beauclerk likened him, for all the world, to the stork in Raphael's cartoon of The Miraculous Draught.† One of Beauclerk's happiest hits, and cer-

---

* Rochester, in his immortal epigram, had said the same of King Charles II.

† This neat descriptive stroke has been attributed also to Richard Paget.

tainly his boldest, was made while Johnson was being congratulated upon his pension. "How much now it was to be hoped," whispered the young blood, in reference to Falstaff's celebrated vow, "that he would purge and live cleanly, as a gentleman should do!" Johnson seems to have taken the hint in good-humor, and actually to have profited by it.

Very soon after leaving Oxford, Beauclerk became engaged to a Miss Draycott, whose family were well known to that affable blue-stocking, Mrs. Montagu; but some coldness on his part, some sensitiveness on hers, broke off the match. His fortune-hunting parent is said to have been disappointed, as the lady owned several lead-mines in her own right. That same year, with Bennet Langton for companion part of the way, Beauclerk, whose health, never robust, now began to give him anxiety, set out on a Continental tour. Baretti, whom he had met at home, received him most kindly at Milan, thanks to Johnson's urgent and friendly letter. By his subsequent knowledge of Italian popular customs, he was able to testify in Baretti's favor, when the latter was under arrest for killing his man in the Haymarket, and in concert with Burke, Garrick, Goldsmith, and Johnson, to help him, in a very interesting case, towards his acquittal. It was reported to Selwyn that the handsome gambling Inglese was robbed at Venice of £10,000! an incident which, perhaps, shortened his peregrinations. If the report were accurate, it would prove that he could have been in no immediate need of pecuniary rescue from his leaden sweetheart. It was Dr. Johnson's opinion, coinciding with the opinion of Roger Ascham on the same general subject, that travel adds very little to one's mental forces, and that Beauclerk might have learned more in the Academe of "Fleet Street, sir!"

Topham Beauclerk married Lady Diana Spencer, the eldest daughter of the second Duke of Marlborough, as soon as she obtained a divorce from her first husband. This was Frederick, Lord Bolingbroke, nephew and heir of the great owner of that title; a very trying gentleman, who was the restless "Bully" of Selwyn's correspondence; he survived until 1787. The ceremony took place March 12, 1768, in St. George's, Hanover Square, "by license of the Archbishop of Canterbury," both conspirators being then residents of the parish. Lady Diana Spencer was born in the spring of 1734, and was therefore in her thirty-fifth year, while Beauclerk was but twenty-nine.* Johnson was disturbed, and felt offended at first with the whole affair; but he never withdrew from the agreeable society of Beauclerk's wife. It is nothing wonderful that the courtship and honey-moon was signalized by the forfeit of Beauclerk's place in the exacting Club, "for continued inattendance," and not regained for a considerable period. "They are in town,

* The register of St. George's betrays a little eager blunder of Lady Di's which is amusing. When the officiating curate asked her to sign, she wrote "Diana Beauclerk," and was obliged to cross out the signature—one knows with what a smile and a flush !—and substitute the "Diana Spencer" which stands beside it.

at Topham's house, and give dinners," one of George Selwyn's gossiping friends wrote, after the wedding. "Lord Ancram dined there yesterday, and called her nothing but Lady Bolingbroke the whole time!" Let us hope that "Milady Bully" triumphed over her awkward guest, and looked, as Earl March once described her under other difficulties, "handsomer than ever I saw her, and not the least abashed;" or as deliberately easy as when she entertained with her gay talk the nervous Boswell who awaited the news of his election or rejection from the Club. She was a blond goddess, exceedingly fair to see. In her middle age she fell under the observant glance of delightful Fanny Burney, who did not fail to allow her "pleasing remains of beauty."

The *divorcée* was fond of and faithful to her new lord, and no drawback upon his æsthetic pride, inasmuch as she was an artist of no mean merit. Horace Walpole built a room for the reception of some of her drawings, which he called his Beauclerk Closet, "not to be shown to all the profane that come to see the house," and he always praised them extravagantly. It is surer critical testimony in her favor that her name figures yet in encyclopædias, and that Sir Joshua, the honest and unbought judge, much admired her work, which Bartolozzi was kept busy engraving. It was her series of illustrations to Bürger's wild ballad of *Leonora* (with the dolly knight, the wooden monks, the genteel heroine, and the vigorous spectres) which, long after, helped to fire the young imagination of Shelley. It is to be feared that her invaluable portrait of Samuel Johnson is not, or never was, extant. "Johnson was confined for some days in the Isle of Skye," writes her rogue of a spouse, "and we hear that he was obliged to swim over to the mainland, taking hold of a cow's tail. . . . Lady Di has promised to make a drawing of it." Sir Joshua's pretty "Una" is the little Elizabeth, afterwards Countess of Pembroke, elder daughter of Lady Di and Topham Beauclerk, painted the year her father died.

The family lived in princely style,

both at their "summer quarters" at Muswell Hill, and on Great Russell Street, where the library, set in a great garden, reached, as Walpole mischievously gauged it, "half-way to Highgate." Lady Di, an admirable hostess, proved herself one of those odd and rare women who take to their husbands' old friends. Selwyn she cordially liked, and her warmest welcome attended Langton, whom she would rally for his remissness, when he failed to come to them at Richmond. He could reach them so easily! she said; all he need do was to lay himself at length, his feet in London and his head with them, *eodem die*. This Richmond home remained her residence during her widowhood. Walpole mentions a Thames boat-race in 1791, when he sat in a tent "just before Lady Di's windows," and gazed upon "a scene that only Richmond, on earth, can exhibit." In the church of the same leafy town her body rests.

Beauclerk died at his Great Russell Street house on March 11, 1780. He had been failing steadily under visitations of his old trouble since 1777, when he lay sick unto death at Bath, and when his wife nursed him tenderly into what seemed to Walpole a miraculous recovery. He was but forty-one years old, and, for all his genius, left no more trace behind than that Persian prince who suddenly disappeared in the shape of a butterfly, and whom old Burton calls a "light phantastick fellow." His air of boyish promise, quite unconsciously worn, hoodwinked his friends into prophecies of his fame. He did not give events a chance to put immortality on his "bright, unbowed, insubmissive head." Yet he was bitterly mourned. "I would walk to the extent of the diameter of the earth to save him," cried Johnson, who had loved him for over twenty years; and again, to Lord Althorp: "This is a loss, sir, that perhaps the whole nation could not repair." Boswell mentions the Doctor's April stroll, at this time, while he was writing his *Lives of the Poets;* and tells us how, returning from a call on the widow of the companion of his youth, David Garrick, he leaned over the rails of the Adelphi Terrace, watching the dark river, and thinking of "two such friends as cannot be supplied." " Poor dear Beauclerk!" Johnson wrote, when his violent grief had somewhat subsided, "*nec, ut soles, dabis joca!* His wit and his folly, his acuteness and his maliciousness, his merriment and his reasoning, are alike over. Such another will not often be found among mankind." Beyond this well-known and characteristic summing-up, the Doctor made no discoverable mention, in his correspondence, of his bereavement, certainly not to the highly-prejudiced Mrs. Thrale, to whom he wrote often and gayly in the year of Beauclerk's death. Nor shall we know how the catastrophe affected Bennet Langton; for all the most interesting papers relating to him were destroyed when the old Hall at Langton-by-Spilsby was burned in 1855. On this subject, as on others as intimate, he stands, perforce, silent.

Readers may recall a passage in Miss Burney's *Diary* which gives countenance to an accusation not borne out by any other testimony, that Beauclerk and his wife had not lived happily together. Dining at Sir Joshua's at Richmond, in 1782, Edmund Burke, sitting next the author of *Evelina*, took occasion, on catching sight of Lady Di's "pretty white house" through the trees, to rejoice in the fact that she was well-housed, moneyed, and a widow. He added that he had never enjoyed the good-fortune of another so keenly as in this blessed instance. Then, turning to his new acquaintance, as the least likely to be informed of the matter, he spoke in his own "strong and marked expressions" of the singular ill-treatment Beauclerk had shown his wife, and the "necessary relief" it must have been to her when he was called away. The statement does not seem to have been gainsaid by any of the company; nor was Burke liable to a slanderous error. So severe a comment on Beauclerk, resting, even as it does, wholly on Miss Burney's veracity, ought, in fairness, to be incorporated into any sketch of the man. On the other side, it is pleasant to discover that Beauclerk, in his will, made five days before the end, bequeathed all he possessed to his wife, and reverted to her the estates of his children, should they die under age. There was but one bequest beyond these, and that was to Thomas Clarke, the faithful valet. The executors named were Lady Di and her brother, Lord Charles Spencer, who had also been groomsman at the marriage, which, despite Burke and its own evil beginnings, it is hard to think of as ill-starred. The joint guardians of Charles George Beauclerk, the only son, were to be Bennet Langton and a Mr. Loyrester, whom Dr. Johnson speaks of as " Leicester, Beauclerk's relation, and a man of good character;" but the guardianship, provisional in case of Lady Di's decease, never came into force, as she survived, in fullest harmony with her three children, up to August 1, 1808, having entered her seventy-fifth year. Various private legacies came to Langton, by his old comrade's dying wish, the most precious among them, perhaps, being the fine Reynolds portrait of Johnson, which had been painted at Beauclerk's cost. Under it was inscribed:

" Ingenium ingens
Inculto latet hoc sub corpore."

Langton thoughtfully effaced the lines. "It was kind of you to take it off," said the burly Doctor, with a sigh; and then (for how could he but recall the contrast of temperament in the two, as well as the affectionate context of Horace?), "not unkind in him to have put it on." The collection of thirty thousand glorious books "*pernobilis Angli T. Beauclerk*" was sold at auction. The advertisement alone is royal reading. There is much amiable witness to the circumstance that Beauclerk was not only an admirer but a buyer of his friends' works. From some kind busybody who attended the twenty-ninth day of the sale, and pencilled his observations upon the margins of the catalogue now in the British Museum, we learn that Goldsmith's *History of the Earth and Animated Nature* (nothing less!), which was issued, with cuts, in the year he died, was knocked down to the vulgar for two and threepence. The shelves, naturally, were stocked with Johnsons. Things dear to the bibliophile were there: innumerable first editions, black-letter, mediæval manuscript, Elzevirs, priceless English and Italian classics, gathered with real feeling and pride; but the most vivid personal interest belonged to the unpretending Lot 3444, otherwise known to fame as *The Rambler*, printed at Edinburgh in 1751; for that was the young Beauclerk's own copy, carried with him to Oxford, and with a fragrance, as of a last century garden, of the first hearty friendship of boys. One cannot help wishing that a sentimental fate left it in Langton's own hands.

Lady Beauclerk, Topham's mother, had died in 1766; and he asked to be buried beside her, or at her feet, in the old chapel of Garston, near Liverpool: "an instance of tenderness," said Johnson, "which I should hardly have expected." There, in the place of his choice, he rests, without an epitaph.

After this the Doctor consoled himself more than ever with Bennet Langton, and with the atmosphere of love and reverence which surrounded him in Langton's house. He had been of old the most desired of all guests at the family seat in Lincolnshire. "Langton, sir!" as he liked to announce, "had a grant of warren from Henry II.; and Cardinal Stephen Langton, of King John's reign, was of this family." Peregrine Langton, Bennet's uncle, was a man of simple and benevolent habits, who brought economy to a science, without niggardliness, and whom Johnson declared to be one of those he clung to at once, both by instinct and reason; Bennet's father, learned, good, and unaffected, the prototype of his learned, good, and unaffected son, was, however, a more diverting character. He had sincerest esteem for Johnson, but looked askance on him for his liberal views, and suspected him, indeed, of being a Papist in secret! He once offered the Doctor a living of some value in the neighborhood, with the suggestion that he should qualify himself for Orders: a chance gravely refused. Of this exemplary but rather archaic squire, Johnson, a dissector of everything he loved, said: "Sir! he is so exuberant a talker in public meetings that the gentlemen of his county are afraid of him. No business can be done for his declamation." In his behalf, too, Johnson produced one of his most astounding words; for having understood that both Mr. and Mrs. Langton were averse to having their portraits taken, he observed aloud that "a superstitious reluctance to sit for one's picture is among the anfractuosities of the human mind."

Bennet Langton married, on the 24th of May, 1770, Mary Lloyd, daughter of the Countess of Haddington, and widow of John, the eighth Earl of Rothes, the stern soldier in laced waistcoat and breastplate beneath, painted by Sir Joshua. It was a common saying at the time that everybody was welcome to a Countess Dowager of Rothes; for it did so happen that three ladies bearing that title were all remarried within a few years. Lady Rothes, although a native of Suffolk, had acquired from long residence in Scotland the accent of that country, which Dr. Johnson bore with magnanimously, on the consideration that it was not indigenous. She had a handsome presence, full of easy dignity, and a naturalness marked enough in the heyday of Georgian affectation. With a vivacity very different from Lady Di Beauclerk's, she kept herself the spring and centre of Langton's tranquil domestic circle: a more womanly woman historiographers cannot find. His own charm of character, after his marriage, slipped more and more into the underground channels of home-life, and so coursed on beneficently in silence. Their children were no fewer than nine,* "not a plain face nor faulty person among them:" the goddess daughters six feet in height, and the three sons so like their Maypole father that they were able once to amuse the Parisians by raising their arms to let a crowd pass. Langton was wont to repeat with some glee certain jests about his height, and Dr. Johnson's nickname of "Lanky" he took ever with excellent grace; and when Garrick had leaped upon a chair to shake hands with him, in old days, he had knelt, at parting, to shake hands with Garrick. But the King's

* Miss Hawkins says "ten," and may have had the extra adopted child in mind.

awkward digs at his "long legs" he found terribly distasteful, nor was he thereby disposed to agree with the Doctor's enthusiastic proclamation, after the famous interview of 1767, that George III. was "as fine a gentleman as Charles II."

It was his cherished plan to educate his boys and girls at home, and to give them a thorough acquaintance with the learned languages. No social engagements were to stand in the way of this prime exigency. He was in great haste to turn his young brood into Masters and Mistresses of Arts. Johnson complained to Miss Burney, as they were both taking tea at Mrs. Thrale's, that nothing would serve Langton but to stand them up before company, and get them to repeat a fable or the Hebrew alphabet, supplying every other word himself, and blushing with pride at the vicarious learning of his infants. But another of the tedious royal jokes, "How does Education go on?" actually lessened his devotion to his self-set task, and worried him like the water-drop in the story, which fell forever on a criminal's head until it had drilled his brain. Again, both he and his wife, even after they had moved into the retirement of Great George Street, Westminster, in pursuance of their design, were far too agreeable and too accessible to be spared the incursions of society. In a word, Minerva found her seat shaken, and her altar-fires not very well tended, and therefore withdrew. Langton impressed one axiom on his young scholars which they never forgot: "Next best to knowing is to be sensible that you do not know." An entirely superfluous waif of a baby was once left at the doors of this same many-childrened house, to be fed, clothed, and petted by Mr. Bennet Langton and Lady Rothes, without protest. Dr. Johnson, who made friends with all children, was especially attached to their third girl, his goddaughter, whom he called "pretty Mrs. Jane," and "my own little Jenny." The very last year of his life her "most humble servant" sent her a loving letter, extant yet, and written purposely in a large round hand as clear as print.

"Langton's children are very pretty,"

Johnson wrote to Boswell in 1777, "and his lady loses her Scotch." But again, during the same year, condescendingly: " I dined lately with poor dear Langton. I do not think he goes on well. His table is rather coarse, and he has his children too much about him." Boswell takes occasion, in reproducing this censure, to reprehend the custom of introducing the children after dinner: a parental indulgence to which he, at least, was not addicted. The Doctor gave him a mild nudge on the subject in remarking later: "I left Langton in London. He has been down with the militia, and is again quiet at home, talking to his little people, as I suppose you do sometimes." While Langton was in camp on Warley Common, in command of the Lincolnshire troops, Johnson spent with him five delightful days, admiring his tall captain's blossoming energies, and poking about curiously among the tents. Langton had fallen, little by little, into a confirmed extravagance, so that the moral of Uncle Peregrine's sagacious living bade fair to be lost upon him. Boswell had a quarrel with Johnson on the subject of Langton's expenditure, during the course of which, according to his own report, the Laird of Auchinleck suffered a "horrible shock" by being told that the best way to drive Langton out of his costly house would be to put him (Boswell) into it. The Doctor was truly concerned, nevertheless, about his engaging spendthrift; up to the very end, he would implore him to keep account-books, even if he had to omit his Aristophanes. "He complains of the ill effects of habit," grumbled the great moralizer, "and he rests content upon a confessed indolence. He told his father himself that he had 'no turn for economy!' but a thief might as well plead that he had no turn for honesty." Such were the hard hits sacred to those Dr. Johnson most esteemed. It transpires from his will that, by way of discouragement, he had lent Langton £750.*

* It is a pity he did not live to read the jolly *American Ballad of Bon Gaultier*, which seems to have a sort of muddled clairvoyant knowledge of this transaction:

"Every day the huge Cawana
Lifted up its monstrous jaws;

In the winter of 1785, Langton came from the country, and took lodgings in Fleet Street, in order to sit beside Johnson as he lay dying, and hold his hand. Nor was he alone in his pious offices: the Hooles, Mr. Sestre, and several others were there, to keep constant vigil. Miss Burney met Langton in the passage December 11th, two days before the end: "He could not," she wrote in her journal, "look at me, nor I at him." But through the foggy and restless nights when Johnson tried to cheer himself, like More and Master William Lilly, by translating into Latin some epigrams from the *Anthologia*, the true Grecian beside him must have been his chief comfort. One can picture the old eyes turning to him for sympathy, perhaps with that same murmured "Lanky!" on awaking, which Boswell laughed to hear from him one merry

> And it swallowed Langton Bennet, (!)
> And digested Rufus Dawes.
>
> "Riled, I ween, was Philip Slingsby
> Their untimely deaths to hear;
> For one author owed him money, (!)
> And the other loved him dear."

Hebridean morning, twelve years before. The last summons did not come in Langton's presence. Hurrying over to Bolt Court at eight of the fatal evening, he was told that all was over three-quarters of an hour ago. That large soul had gone away, as Leigh Hunt so beautifully said of Coleridge, "to an infinitude hardly wider than his thoughts." Then Langton, who was wont to shape his words with grace and ease, went up-stairs, and tried to pen a letter to Boswell, which is more touching than tears: "I am now sitting in the room where his venerable remains exhibit a spectacle, the interesting solemnity of which, difficult as it would be in any sort to find terms to express, so to you, my dear sir, whose sensations will paint it so strongly, it would be of all men the most superfluous to"—and there, hopelessly choked and confused, it broke off.

Langton bore Johnson's pall; and he succeeded him as Professor of Ancient Literature in the Royal Academy, as Gibbon had replaced Goldsmith in the chair of Ancient History. He survived many years, the delight of his company to the last. He, like others, was given in his later years to detailing anecdotes of his great friend, with an approximation to that friend's manner. One lady critic, at least, thought that these explosive imitations did not become "his own serious and respectable character." On December 18, 1801, in Anspach Place, Southampton, a venerable nook "between the walls and the sea," when Wordsworth, Scott, and Coleridge were yet in their unheralded prime, when Charles Lamb was twenty-six, Byron a dreaming boy on the Cotswold hills, and Keats and Shelley little fair-eyed children, gentle Bennet Langton, known to none of these, and somewhat forgotten as a loiterer from the march of a glorious yesterday, slipped out of life. "I am persuaded," wrote one who knew him well, "that all his inactivity, all the repugnance he showed to putting on the harness of this world's toil, arose from the spirituality of his frame of mind . . . I believe his mind was in Heaven, wheresoever he corporeally existed." He was laid under the chancel of ancient St. Michael's at Southampton, with Johnson's fond benison, "Be my soul with Langton's!" inscribed on the marble tablet above him.* The Rev. John Wooll of Midhurst, Joseph Warton's editor, was one of the few present at the funeral ceremony, and he leaves us to infer that it had a rather neglectful privacy, not, indeed, out of keeping with the "godly, righteous, and sober life" it closed. Langton's will, drawn up in the June of 1800, and preserved in Somerset House, devised to the sole executrix, his "dear wife," who outlived him by nearly twenty years, his real and personal estate, his books, his wines, his prints, his horses, and, as a gift particularly pretty, his right of navigation in the river Wey. George Langton was separately provided for, but there were some £8000 for the eight younger children. The document is crowded with technical details, and very long; and the manifest inference, on the whole, is that the dear

* The church has since been "restored," and the fine epitaph is now (1890) "skyed" on the south wall of the nave.

squire's affairs were in a prodigious tangle. There is no wish expressed concerning his burial, and, what is more curious, there are no Christian formulas for the committal of the *animula vagula blandula:* a lack perhaps not to be wondered at in Beauclerk's concise testament, but somewhat notable in the case of a person who certainly had a soul.

So went Beauclerk first of the three, Langton last, with the good ghost still between them, as he in his homespun, they in their flowered velvet, had walked many a year together on this earth. The old companionship had undergone some sorry changes ere it fell utterly to dust and ashes. Its happy prime had been in the Oxford " Longs," when the Doctor humored his lads, and tented under their roofs, plucking flowers at one house, and romping with dogs at the other; or in 1764, at the starting of the immortal Club, when the two of its founders, who had no valid or pretended claim to celebrity, perched on the sills like useful genii, with a mission to overrule sluggish melancholy, and renew the sparkle in abstracted eyes. How supereminently they did what they chose to do, and what vagaries they roused out of Johnson's profound hypochondria! Did not Topham Beauclerk's mother once have to reprove that august author for a suggestion to seize some pleasure-grounds which they were passing in a carriage? " Putting such things into young people's heads !" said she. Where could the innocent Beauclerk's elbow have been at that moment, contrary to the canons of polite society, but in the innocent Langton's ribs? The gray reprobate, so censured, explained to Boswell: "Lady Beauclerk has no notion of a joke, sir! She came late into life, and has a mighty unpliable understanding." Who can forget the Doctor's visit to Beauclerk at Windsor, when, falling into the clutches of that gamesome and ungodly youth, he was beguiled from church-going of a fine Sunday morning, and strolled about outside, talking and laughing during sermon-time, and finally spread himself at length on a mossy tomb, only to be told, with a giggle and a pleased rub of the hands, that he was as bad as Hogarth's Idle Apprentice? Or the other visit in the north, when, after ceremoniously relieving his pockets of keys, knife, pencil, and purse, Samuel Johnson, LL.D., deliberately rolled down a hill, and landed, betumbled out of all recognition, at the bottom? Langton had tried to dissuade him, for the incline was very steep, and the candidate scarcely of the requisite suppleness. "Oh, but I haven't had a roll for such a long time!" pleaded his unanswerable big guest.

Best of all, we have the history of that memorable morning when Beauclerk and Langton, having supped together at a city tavern, roused Johnson at three o'clock at his Inner Temple Lane Chambers, and brought him to the door, fearful but aggressive, in his shirt and his little dark wig, and his slippers down at the heels, armed with a poker. "What! and is it YOU? Faith, I'll have a frisk with you, ye young dogs!" We have visions of the Covent Garden inn, and the great brimming bowl, with Lord Lansdowne's drinking-song for grace; the hucksters and fruiterers staring at the strange central figure, always sure to gather a mob, even during the moment he would stand by a lady's coach-door in Fleet Street; the merry boat going its way by oar to Billingsgate, its mad crew bantering the watermen on the river; and two of the roisterers (equally wild, despite a little chronological disparity of thirty years or so) scolding the other for hastening off, on an afternoon appointment, "to dine with wretched unidea'd girls!" What golden vagabondism! "I heard of your frolic t'other night; you'll be in *The Chronicle!* .... I shall have my old friend to bail out of the round-house!" said Garrick. "As for Garrick, sirs," tittered the pious Johnson aside to his accomplices, "he dare not do such a thing. His wife would not let him!" All this mirth and whim sweetened the Doctor's heavy life. He had other intimates, other disciples. But these were Gay Heart and Gentle Heart, who drove his own blue-devils away with their idolatrous devotion, and whose bearing towards him stands ever as the best possible corroboration of his great and warm nature. With him and for him, they so fill the air of the time that to whomsoever has but thought of them that hour, London must seem lonely without their idyllic figures.

—"Our day is gone:
Clouds, dews, and dangers come; our deeds are done."

There are gods as good for the after-years; but Odin is down, and his pair of unreturning birds have flown west and east.

V
WILLIAM HAZLITT
1778–1830

WILLIAM HAZLITT

HE titles of William Hazlitt's first books bear witness to the ethic spirit in which he began life. From his beloved father, an Irish dissenting minister, he inherited his unworldliness, his obstinacy, his love of inexpedient truth, and his interest in the emancipation and well-being of his fellow-creatures. Bred in an air of seriousness and integrity, the child of twelve announced by post that he had spent "a very agreeable day" reading one hundred and sixty pages of Priestley, and hearing two good sermons. A year later he appeared, under a Greek signature, in *The Shrewsbury Chronicle*, protesting against sectarian injustice; an infant herald in the great modern movement towards fair play. The roll of the portentous periods must

have made his father weep for pride and diversion. William's young head was full of moral philosophy and jurisprudence, and he had what is the top of luxury for one of his temperament: perfect license of mental growth. Alone with his parents (one of whom was always a student and a recluse), and for the most part without the school-fellows who are likely to adjust the perilous effects of books, he became choked with theories, and thought more of the needful repeal of the Test Act than of his breakfast. He found his way at fourteen into the Unitarian College at Hackney, but eventually broke from his traces, saving his fatherland from the spectacle of a unique theologian. During the year 1795 he saw the pictures at Burleigh House, and began to live. Desultory but deep study, at home and near home, took up the time before his first leisurely choice of a profession. His lonely broodings, his early love for Miss Railton, his four enthusiastic months at the Louvre, his silent friendship with Wordsworth and with Coleridge; the country walks, the pages and prints, the glad tears of his youth,—these were the fantastic tutors which formed him; nor had he ever much respect for any other kind of training. The lesson he prized most was the lesson straight from life and nature. He comments, tartly enough, on the sophism that observation in idleness, or the growth of bodily skill and social address, or the search for the secret of honorable power over people, is not in any wise to be accounted as learning. Montaigne, who was in Hazlitt's ancestral line, was of this mind: "*Ce qu'on sçait droictement, on en dispose sans regarder au patron, sans tourner les yeulx vers son livre.*" Hazlitt insists, too, that learned men are but "the cisterns, not the fountain-heads, of knowledge." He hated the schoolmaster, and has said as witty things of him as Mr. Oscar Wilde. Yet his little portrait-study of the mere book-worm, in *The Conversation of Authors*, has a never-to-be-forgotten sweetness. His mental nurture was serviceable; it was of his own choosing; it fitted him for the work he had to do. Like Marcus Aurelius, he congratulated himself that he did not squander his youth "chopping logic and scouring the heavens." Hazlitt once entered upon an *Inquiry whether the Fine Arts are promoted by Academies;* the answer, from him, is readily anticipated.

"If arts and schools reply,"

he might have added,—and it is a wonder that he did not,

"Give arts and schools the lie!"

Mr. Matthew Arnold made a famous essay on the same topic, and some readers recollect distinctly that his verdict, for England, would be in the affirmative, whereas it was no such matter. Now, no man can conceive of Hazlitt presenting both sides of a case so impartially as to be misunderstood, especially upon so vital a subject. He pastured, he was not trained; and therefore he would have you and your children's children scoff at universities. Indeed, though the boy's lack of discipline told on him all through life, his reader regrets nothing else which a university could have given him, except, perhaps, milder manners. Hazlitt was perfectly aware that he had too little general knowledge; but general knowledge he did not consider so good a tool for his self-set task in life as a persistent, passionate study of one or two subjects. Again, he is pleased to conjecture, with bluntness, that if he had learned more he would have thought less. (Perhaps he was the friend cited by Elia, who gave up reading to improve his originality! He was certainly useful to Elia in delicate and curious ways: a whole vein of rich eccentricity ready for that sweet philosopher's working.) Hear him pronouncing upon himself at the very end: "I have, then, given proof of some talent and more honesty; if there is haste and want of method, there is no commonplace, nor a line that licks the dust. If I do not appear to more advantage, I at least appear such as I am." Divorce that remark and the truth of it from Hazlitt, and there is no Hazlitt left. He stood for individualism. He wrote from what was, in the highest degree for his purpose, a full mind, and with that blameless conscious superiority which a full mind must needs feel in this empty world. His whole intellectual stand is taken on the positive and concrete side of things. He has a fine barbaric cocksureness; he dwells not with althoughs and neverthelesses, like Mr. Symonds and Mr. Saintsbury. "I am not one of those," he says, concerning Edmund Kean's first appearance in London, "who, when they see the sun breaking from behind a cloud, stop to inquire whether it is the moon." And he takes enormous interest in his own promulgation, because it is inevitably not only what he thinks, but what he has long thought. He delivers an opinion with the air proper to a host who is master of a vineyard, and can furnish name and date to every flagon he unseals.

None of Hazlitt's energies went to waste: he earned his soul early, and how proud he was of the possession! Retrospection became his forward horizon. He was all aglow at the thought of that beatific yesterday; in his every mood "the years that are fled knock at the door, and enter." He struggled no more thereafter, having fixed his beliefs and found his voice. He saw no occasion to change. "As to myself," he wrote at fifty, referring to Lamb's well-known "surfeits of admiration" concerning some objects once adored, "as to myself, any one knows where to have me!" He adds: "In matters of taste and feeling, one proof that my conclusions have not been quite shallow or hasty is the circumstance of their having been lasting.... This continuity of impression is the only thing on which I pride myself." A fine saying in the *Boswell Redivivus*, attributed to Opie, is as clearly expressed elsewhere by Hazlitt's self: that a man in his lifetime can do but one thing; that there is but one effort and one victory, and all the rest is as machinery in motion. "What I write costs me nothing, but it cost me a great deal twenty years ago. I have added little to my stock since then, and taken little from it." His sensations, latterly, were "July shoots," graftings on the old sap. It is his boast in almost his final essay that his tenacious brain holds fast while the planets are turning. He can look at a child's kite in heaven, to the last, with the eyes of a child: " It pulls at my heart."

His conservative habit, however, seemed to teach him everything by inference. In 1821, familiar with none of the elder dramatists save Shakespeare, he borrowed their folios, and shut himself up for six weeks at Winterslow Hut on Salisbury Plain. He returned to town steeped in his theme, and with the beautiful and authoritative *Lectures* written. Appreciation of the great Elizabethans is common enough now; seventy years ago, propagated by Lamb's *Specimens*, 1808, it was the business only of adventurers and pioneers. Here is a critic indeed who, without a suspicion of audacity, can arise as a stranger to arraign the *Arcadia*, and "shake hands with Signor Orlando Friscobaldo as the oldest acquaintance" he has! The thing, exceptional as it was, proves that William Hazlitt knew his resources. His devoted friend Patmore attributes his "unpremeditated art," terse, profound, original, and always moving at full speed, to two facts: "first, that he never, by choice, wrote on any topic or question in which he did not, for some reason or other, feel a deep personal interest; and, secondly, because on all questions on which he did so feel, he had thought, meditated, and pondered, in the silence and solitude of his own heart, for years and years before he ever contemplated doing more than thinking of them." Unlike a distinguished historian, who, according to Horace Walpole, " never understood anything until he had written of it," Hazlitt brought to his every task a mind violently made up, and a vocation for special pleading which nothing could withstand.

Sure as he is, he means to be nobody's hired guide: a resolve for which the general reader cannot be too grateful. In wilful and mellow study of what chance threw in his way his strength grew, and his limitations with it. It is small wonder that he hated schoolmasters, and the public which expected of him schoolmaster platitudes. He had a pride of intellect not unlike Rousseau's, and he seems to have had ever in mind Rousseau's cardinal declaration that if he were no better than other men, he was at least different from them. Hazlitt defined his own functions with proper haughtiness, in the amusing apology of *Capacity and Genius*. "I was once applied to, in a delicate emergency, to write an article on a difficult subject for an encyclopædia; and was advised to take time, and give it a systematic and scientific form; to avail myself of all the knowledge that was to be obtained upon the subject, and arrange it with clearness and method. I made answer that, as to the first, I *had* taken time to do all that I ever pretended to do, as I had thought incessantly on different matters for twenty years of my life; that I had no particular knowledge of the subject in question, and no head for arrangement; that the utmost I could do, in such a case, would be, when a systematic and scientific article was prepared, to write marginal notes upon it, to insert a remark or illustration of my own (not to be found in former encyclopædias!) or to suggest a better definition than had been offered in the text."* Such independence nobly became him, and none the less because it kept him poor. But in the course of time, he had to work, and keep on working, under wretched disadvantages. He had spurts of revolt, after long experience of compulsory composition; his darling wish in 1822 (confided to his wife, of all persons) being that he "could marry some woman with a good fortune, that he might not be under the necessity of writing another line!"

There was in him absolutely nothing of the antiquary and the scholar, as the modern world understands those most serviceable gentlemen. He was a "surveyor," as he said, erroneously, of Bacon. He was continuously drawn into the byway, and ever in search of the accidental, the occult; he lusted, like Sir Thomas Browne, to find the great meanings of minor things. The "pompous big-wigs" of his day, as Thackeray called them, hated his informality, his boldly novel methods, his vivacity and enthusiasm.

* The article on *The Fine Arts* in the *Encyclopædia Britannica* is signed "W. H."

He had, within proscribed bounds, an exquisite and affectionate curiosity, like that of the Renaissance. "The invention of a fable is to me the most enviable exertion of human genius: it is the discovery of a truth to which there is no clew, and which, when once found out, can never be forgotten." "If the world were good for nothing else, it would be a fine subject for speculation." It is his deliberate dictum that it were "worth a life" to sit down by an Italian wayside, and work out the reason why the Italian supremacy in art has always been along the line of color, not along the line of form.

He depended so entirely upon his memory that those who knew him best say that he never took notes, neither in gallery, library, nor theatre; yet his inaccuracies are few and slight,* and he must have secured by this habit a prodigious

* Mrs. Hazlitt the first, it would appear, undertook to verify her husband's quotations for him. His favorite metaphor, "Like the tide which flows on to the Propontic, and knows no ebb," must have passed many times under her eye. Any reference to Othello himself, in the great scene of Act III., would have shown four lines for William Hazlitt's explicit one.

freedom and luxury in the act of writing. He would rather stumble than walk according to rule; and he was so pleasantly beguiled with some of his own images (that, for instance, of immortality the bride of the youthful spirit, and of the procession of camels seen across the distance of three thousand years) that he reiterates them upon every fit occasion. He cites, twice and thrice, the same passages from the Elizabethans. He is a masterly quoter, and lingers like a suitor upon the borders of old poesy. His infallibility, like the Pope's, is of narrow scope and nicely defined. When he steps beyond his accustomed tracks, which is seldom, his vagaries are entertaining. You may account for his declaration that Thomas Warton's sonnets rank as the very best in the language, by reflecting that he dealt not in sonnets and knew nothing of them; if he prefer *Hercules Raging* to any other Greek tragedy, it is collateral proof that he was no wide-travelled Grecian, nor even Euripideian; when he gives his distinguished preference to Shakespeare's Helena, there is small need of adding that Mr. Hazlitt, albeit with an affectionate friendship for Mary Lamb, with a mother, a sister, a dynasty of sweethearts, and two wives, was notoriously unlearned in women.*

The events of his life count for so little that they are hardly worth recording. He was born into a high-principled and intelligent family, at Mitre Lane, Maidstone, Kent, on the 10th of April, in the year 1778. His infancy was passed there and in Ireland, his boyhood in New England and in Shropshire. Prior to a long visit to Paris, where he made some noble copies of Titian, he came in 1802 to Bloomsbury, where his elder brother John, an advanced Liberal in politics and an excellent miniature-painter, had a studio; and here he worked at art for several joyous years, finally abandoning it for literature. The portraits he painted, utterly lacking in grace, are fraught with

---

* Some of Hazlitt's comments on women are full of unconscious humor. In *Great and Little Things* he admits being snubbed by the fair, and adds with grandiloquence: "I took a pride in my disgrace, and concluded that I had elsewhere my inheritance!"

power and meaning; few of these are
extant, thanks to the fading and cracking pigments of the modern schools.
The old Manchester woman in shadow,
done in 1803, and the head of his father,
dating from a twelvemonth later (two
things to which Hazlitt makes memorable reference in his essays), are no longer
distinguishable, save to a very patient
eye, upon the blackened canvases in his
grandson's possession. The picture of
the child Hartley Coleridge, begun at the
Lakes in 1802, has perished from the
damp; that of Charles Lamb in the Venetian doublet survives since 1804, in its
serious and primitive browns,* as the
best-known example of an English artist
not in the catalogues. Its historic value,
however, is not superior to that of two
portraits of Hazlitt himself: one a study
in strong light and shade, with a wreath
upon the head, now very much time-eaten; and another representing him at
about the age of twenty-five, with a three-quarters front face looking over the right

* In the National Portrait Gallery, London.

shoulder, which appeals to the spectator like spoken truth. It is all but void of the beauty characterizing the striking Bewick head (especially as retouched and reproduced in Mr. Alexander Ireland's valuable book of 1889, which is a sort of Hazlitt anthology), and characterizing, no less, John Hazlitt's charming miniatures of William at five and at thirteen; therefore it can deal in no self-flattery. Fortunately, we have from the hand which knew him best the lank, odd, reserved youth in whom great possibilities were brewing; thought and will predominate in this portrait, and it expresses the sincere soul. It would be idle to criticise the technique of a work disowned by its author. Hazlitt had, as we know from much testimony, a most interesting and perplexing face, with the magnificent brow almost belied by shifting eyes, and the petulance and distrust of the mouth and chin; but a face prepossessing on the whole from the clear marble of his complexion,* remarkable in a land of

* *Blackwood's*, in the charming fashion of the time, repeatedly refers to Hazlitt's "pimples"; and Byron

ruddy cheeks. His lonely and peculiar life lent him its own hue; the eager look of one indeed a sufferer, but with the light full upon him of visions and of dreams:

"*Chi pallido si fece sotto l'ombra
Sì di Parnaso, o bevve in sua cisterna?*"

In 1798 Hazlitt had his immortal meeting at Wem with Samuel Taylor Coleridge. He described himself at this period as "dumb, inarticulate, helpless, like a worm by the wayside," striving in vain to put on paper the thoughts which oppressed him, shedding tears of vexation at his inability, and feeling happy if in eight years he could write as many pages. The abiding influence of his First Poet he has acknowledged in an imperishable chapter. For a long while he still kept in "the o'erdarkened ways" of Malthus and Tucker, or in the shadow, dear to

credited and supplemented the allegation. Hazlitt himself says somewhere "that to lay a thing to a person's charge from which he is perfectly free, shows spirit and invention!" The calumny is not worth mention, except as a fair specimen of the journalistic methods against which literary men had to contend some eighty years ago.

him, of Hobbes; but in 1817 the floodgates broke, the pure current gushed out; and in the *Characters of Shakespeare's Plays* we have the primal pledge of Hazlitt as we know him, "such as had never been before him, such as will never be again." From a "dumbness" and diffidence extreme, he developed into the readiest of writers; his sudden pages, year after year, transcribed in his slant large hand, went to the printers rapidly and at first draft. The longer he used his dedicated pen, the freer, the brighter, the serener it grew. In the fourteen or fifteen of his books which deal with genius and the conduct of life, there is, throughout, an indescribable unaffected zest, a self-same and unwavering certitude of handling. Once he learned his trade, he gave himself a large field and an easy rein. He never warmed towards a subject chosen for him. His conversation was non-professional. He considered a discussion as to the likelihood of the weather's holding up for to-morrow as "the end and privilege of a life of study."

In London, as soon as he had abandoned painting, he became a parliamentary reporter, and began to lecture on the English philosophers and metaphysicians. He furnished his famous dramatic criticisms to *The Morning Chronicle*, *The Champion*, *The Examiner*, and *The Times*, and he acted later as home editor of *The Liberal*. He married, on May-day of 1808, Miss Sarah Stoddart, who owned the property near Salisbury where he afterwards spent melancholy years alone. He fulfilled one human duty perfectly, for he loved and reared his son. A most singular infatuation for the unlovely daughter of his landlady; a second inauspicious marriage in 1824 with a Mrs. Isabella Bridgwater; a prolonged journey on the Continent; the failure of the publishers of his *Life of Napoleon*, which thus in his needful days brought him no competence; a long illness heroically borne, and a burial in the parish churchyard of St. Anne's, under a headstone raised, in a romantic remorse after an estrangement, by Charles Wells, the author of *Joseph and his Brethren*,—these round out the meagre details of Hazlitt's life. He died in the arms of his son and of his old friend Charles Lamb,* on the 18th of September, 1830, at 6 Frith Street, Soho.

His domestic experiences, indeed, had been nearly as extraordinary as Shelley's. Sarah Walker, of No. 9 Southampton Buildings, is a sort of burlesque counterpart of that other "spouse, sister, angel," Emilia Viviani. Nothing in literary history is much funnier than Mr. Hazlitt's kind assistance to Mrs. Hazlitt in securing her divorce, going to visit her at Edinburgh, and supplying funds and advice over the teacups, while the process was pending, unless it be Shelley's ingenuous invitation to his deserted young wife to come and dwell forever with himself and Mary! The silent dramatic withdrawal of the second Mrs. Hazlitt, the well-to-do relict of a colonel, who is

* Lamb had been his groomsman twenty-two years before, at the Church of St. Andrew, Holborn, "and like to have been turned out several times during the ceremony; anything awful makes me laugh!" as he confessed in a letter to Southey in 1815.

henceforth swallowed up in complete oblivion, is a feature whose like is missing in Shelley's romance. Events in Hazlitt's path were not many, and his inner calamities seem somehow subordinated to exterior workings. It is not too much to say that to the French Revolution and the white heat of hope it diffused over Europe he owed the renewal of the very impetus within him: his moral probity, his mental vigor, and his physical cheer. His measure of men and things was fixed by its standard. Other enthusiasts wavered and went back to the flesh-pots of Egypt, but not he. *Et cuncta terrarum subacta præter atrocem animum Catonis.* Towards the grandest inconsistency this world has seen, he bore himself with a consistency nothing less than touching. Everywhere, always, as a friend who understood him well reminds a later generation, "Hazlitt was the only man of letters in England who dared openly to stand by the French Revolution, through good and evil report, and who had the magnanimity never to turn his back upon its child and champion." The ruin of

Napoleon, and the final news that "the hunter of greatness and of glory was himself a shade," meant more to him than the relinquishment of his early and cherished art, or the fading of the long dream that his heart "should find a heart to speak to." On his last autumn afternoon, he said what no one else would have dared to say for him: "I have had a happy life." Such it was, if we are to compute happiness by souls, and not by the incidents which befall them. What were the things which atoned to this reformer for the curse of a mind too sentient, a heart never far from breaking? Over and above all amended and amending abuses, the memory of the Rembrandts on the walls of Burleigh House; the waving crest of the Tuderley woods; the sky, the turf, "a winding road, and a three-hours' march to dinner"; the impersonator of Richard III. most to his mind, who lighted the stage, "and fought as if drunk with wounds"; and the figure (how pastoral and tender!) of the shepherd-boy bringing a nest for his young mistress's sky-lark, "not doomed to dip his wings in the dappled dawn." What heresy to the ancients would be this creed of poetic compensation! Montesquieu adhered to it; but hardly from baffled and impassioned Hazlitt, dying in his prime, would the avowal have been expected. Yet he had written almost always, as Jeffrey saw, in "a happy intoxication." Like the sundial, in one of the most charming among his miscellaneous essays, he kept count only of the hours of joy.

Hazlitt's erratic levees among coffeehouse wits and politicians, his slack dress, his rich and fitful talk, his beautiful fierce head, go to make up any accurate impression of the man. Mr. P. G. Patmore has drawn him for us; a strange portrait from a steady hand: in certain moods "an effigy of silence," pale, anxious, emaciated, with an awful look ever and anon, like the thunder-cloud in a clear heaven, sweeping over his features with still fury.* He was so much at the mercy of

* Orrery had seen this same bitter indignation overwhelm Swift at times, "so that it is scarcely possible for human features to carry in them more terror and austerity."

an excitable and extra-sensitive organization that an accidental failure to return his salute upon the street, or, above all, the gaze of a servant as he entered a house, plunged him into an excess of wrath and misery. Full, at other times, of scrupulous good faith and generosity, he would, under the stress of a fancied hurt, say and write malicious things about those he most honored. He must have been a general thorn in the flesh, for he had no tact whatever. "I love Henry," said one of Thoreau's friends, "but I cannot like him." Shy, splenetic, with Dryden's "down look," readier to give than to exchange, Hazlitt was a riddle to strangers' eyes. His deep voice seemed at variance with his gliding step and his glance, bright but sullen; his hand felt as if it were the limp, cold fin of a fish, and was an unlooked-for accompaniment to the fiery soul warring everywhere with darkness, and drenched in altruism. His habit of excessive tea-drinking, like Dr. Johnson's, was to keep down sad thoughts. For sixteen years before he died, from the day on which he formed his resolution, Hazlitt never touched spirits of any kind. Profuse of money when he had it, he lacked heart, says Mr. Patmore, to live well. Wherever he dwelt there was what Carlyle, in Hunt's case, called "tinkerdom"; his marriage, and his residence under the august roof which had been Milton's,* did not mend matters for him. He covered the walls and mantel-pieces of London landladies, after the fashion of the French bohemian painters, with samples of his noblest style; and the savor of yesterday's potions of strong tea exhaled into their curtains. Never was there, despite his confessional attitude, so non-communicative a soul. He never corresponded with anybody; he never would walk arm in arm with anybody; he never, perhaps from horror of the "patron" bogie, dedicated a book to anybody. De Quincey knew a man warmly disposed towards Hazlitt who learned to shudder and dread daggers when poor Hazlitt, with a gesture habitual to him,

* At 19 York Street, Westminster. The house, with its tablet "To the Prince of Poets" set by Hazlitt himself, was destroyed in 1877.

thrust his right hand between the buttons of his waistcoat! And he once cheerfully requested of a cheerful colleague: "Write a character of me for the next number. I want to know why everybody has such a dislike to me." As a social factor he was something atrocious.* The most humane of men, his suspicions and shyings cut him off completely from humanity. The base war waged upon him by the great Tory magazines could not have affected him so deeply that it changed his demeanor towards his fellows; for he had the met-

---

* A snappy unpublished letter to Hunt, sold among the Hazlitt papers at Sotheby, Wilkinson and Hodge's, in the late autumn of 1893, complains bitterly of kind Basil Montagu, who had once put off a proffered visit from Hazlitt, on the ground that a party of other guests was expected. The deterred one was naturally wroth. "Yet after this, I am not to look at him a little *in abstracto!* This is what has soured me and made me sick of friendship and acquaintanceship." Hazlitt confounded cause and effect. He was unwelcome in general gatherings where his genius was unappreciated; and we may be sure Montagu was sorry for it when, in the interests of concord, he held up so deprecating and inhospitable a hand. But among those who nursed Hazlitt in his last illness, Basil Montagu was not the least loyal.

tle of a paladin, which no invective could break. But, alas! he had "the canker at the heart," which is no fosterer of "the rose upon the cheek."

With all this fever and heaviness in Hazlitt's blood, he had a hearty laugh, musical to hear. Haydon, in his exaggerated manner, reports an uncharitable conversation held with him once on the subject of Leigh Hunt in Italy, during which the two misconstruing critics, in their great glee, "made more noise than all the coaches, wagons, and carts outside in Piccadilly." His smile was singularly grave and sweet. Mrs. Shelley wrote, on coming back to England, in her widowhood, and finding him much changed: "His smile brought tears to my eyes; it was like melancholy sunlight on a ruin." A man who sincerely laughs and smiles is somewhat less than half a cynic. If there be any alive at this late hour who questions the genuineness of Hazlitt's high spirits, he may be referred to the essay *On Going a Journey*, with the pæan about "the gentleman in the parlor," in the finest emulation of Cowley; but chiefly and constantly to *The Fight*, with its lingering De-Foe-like details, sprinkled, not in the least ironically, with gold-dust of Chaucer and the later poets: the rich-ringing, unique *Fight*,* predecessor

---

* *The Fight* appeared in the *New Monthly Magazine* in 1822. It was itself antedated by *The Fancy* or John Hamilton Reynolds, Keats's friend and Hood's brother-in-law, which was printed in 1820. The jolly iambics are as inspired as the essay. "P. C." is, of course, Pugilistic Club.

> "Oh, it is life! to see a proud
> And dauntless man step, full of hopes,
> Up to the P. C. stakes and ropes,
> Throw in his hat, and with a spring
> Get gallantly within the ring;
> Eye the wide crown, and walk awhile
> Taking all cheerings with a smile;
> To see him strip; his well-trained form,
> White, glowing, muscular, and warm,
> All beautiful in conscious power,
> Relaxed and quiet, till the hour;
> His glossy and transparent frame,
> In radiant plight to strive for fame!
> To look upon the clean shap'd limb
> In silk and flannel clothèd trim;
> While round the waist the kerchief tied
> Makes the flesh glow in richer pride.
> 'Tis more than life to watch him hold
> His hand forth, tremulous yet bold,
> Over his second's, and to clasp
> His rival's in a quiet grasp;

of Borrow's famous burst about the "all tremendous bruisers" of *Lavengro;* and not to be matched in our peaceful literature save with the eulogy and epitaph of Jack Cavanagh, by the same hand. Divers hints have been circulated, within sixty-odd years, that Mr. Hazlitt was a timid person; also that he had no turn

> To watch the noble attitude
> He takes, the crowd in breathless mood;
> And then to see, with adamant start,
> The muscles set, and the great heart
> Hurl a courageous splendid light
> Into the eye, and then—the FIGHT!"

But this is general: Hazlitt is specific. His particular Fight was the great one between Neate of Bristol and Tom Hickman the Gasman, Neate being the victor. On May 20, 1823, Neate met Spring of Hertfordshire (so translated out of his natural patronymic of Winter), in a contest for the championship, and Neate himself went under. This latter battle was mock-heroically celebrated by Maginn in *Blackwood's*, and Hood's casual meteorological simile heaped up honors on the winner:

> "The Spring! I shrink and shudder at her name.
>   For why? I find her breath a bitter blighter,
>   And suffer from her blows as if they came
>   From Spring the fighter!"

So that literature may be said to have set close to the ropes in those days, from first to last.

for jokes. These ingenious calumnies may be trusted to meet the fate of the Irish pagan fairies, small enough at the start, whose punishment it is to dwindle ever and ever away, and point a moral to succeeding generations. Hazlitt's paradoxes are not of malice prepense, but are the ebullitions both of pure fun and of the truest philosophy. "The only way to be reconciled with old friends is to part with them for good." "Goldsmith had the satisfaction of good-naturedly relieving the necessities of others, and of being harassed to death with his own." "Captain Burney had you at an advantage by never understanding you." Scattered mention of "people who live on their own estates and on other people's ideas"; of Jeremy Bentham, who had been translated into French, "when it was the greatest pity in the world that he had not been translated into English"; of the Coleridge of prose, one of whose prefaces is "a masterpiece of its kind, having neither beginning, middle, nor end"; and even of the "singular animal," John Bull himself, since "being the beast he is has made a man of him":—these are no ill shots at the sarcastic. Congreve, with all his quicksilver wit, could not outgo Hazlitt on Thieves, *videlicet:* "Even a highwayman, in the way of trade, may blow out your brains; but if he uses foul language at the same time, I should say he was no gentleman!" Hazlitt's sense of humor has quality, if not quantity. How was it this same sense of humor, this fine-grained reticence, which wrote, nay, printed, in 1823, the piteous and ludicrous canticle of the goddess Sarah?

Hazlitt was a great pedestrian from his boyhood on, and, like Goldsmith, a fair hand at the game of fives, which he played by the day. Wherever he was, his pocket bulged with a book. It gave him keen pleasure to set down the hour, the place, the mood, and the weather of various ecstatic first readings. He became acquainted with *Love for Love* in a low wainscoted tavern parlor between Farnham and Alton, looking out upon a garden of larkspur, with a portrait of Charles

II. crowning the chimney-piece; in his father's house he fell across *Tom Jones*, "a child's Tom Jones, an innocent creature"; he bought Milton and Burke at Shrewsbury, on the march; he looked up from Mrs. Inchbald's *Simple Story*, when its pathos grew too poignant, to find "a summer shower dropping manna" on his head, and "an old crazy hand-organ playing *Robin Adair*." And on April 10, 1798, his twentieth birthday, he sat down to a volume of the *New Eloïse*, a book which kept its hold upon him, "at the inn of Llangollen, over a bottle of sherry and a cold chicken!" The frank epicurean catalogue, as of equal spiritual and corporeal delight, is worth notice. Do we not know that Mr. Hazlitt had wood-partridges for supper, in his middle age, at the Golden Cross, in Rastadt, near Mayence? Yet he failed to record what book lay by his plate, and distracted his attention from her who had been a widow, and who was already planning her respectable exit from his society. Evidence that he was an eater of taste is to be accumulated eagerly by his partisans, for eating is one of many engaging human characteristics which establish him as lovable — that is, posthumously lovable. Barry Cornwall was so jealously tender of his memory that he would have forbidden any one to write of Hazlitt who had not known him. As he did not warm miscellaneously to everybody, it followed that his friends were few. We do not forget which one of these, during their only difference, thought "to go to his grave without finding, or expecting to find, such another companion."*

Hazlitt would have set himself down, by choice, as a metaphysician. Up to the time when his *Life of Napoleon* was well in hand, he used to affirm that the anonymous *Principles of Human Action*, which he completed at twenty, in the literary style of the azoic age, was his best work. He was rather proud, too, of the *Characteristics in the Manner of Rochefoucauld's Maxims*, his one dreary book, which contains a couple of inductions worthy of Pascal, some sophistries and

* "Lamb, in "*A Letter to R. Southey, Esq.*"

hollow cynicisms not native to Hazlitt's brain, and a vast number of the very professorisms which he scouted. Maxims, indeed, are sown broadcast over his pages, which Alison the historian classified as better to quote than to read; but they gain by being incidental, and embedded in the body of his fancies. His vein of original thought comes nowhere so perfectly into play as in its application to affairs. His pen is anything but abstruse,

"Housed in a dream, at distance from the kind."

He did not recognize that to display his highest power he needed deeds and men, and their tangible outcome to be criticised. His preferences were altogether wed to the past. In his essay on *Envy* he excuses, with a wise reflection, his comparative indifference to living writers: "We try to stifle the sense we have of their merit, not because they are new or modern, but because we are not sure they will ever be old." Or, as Professor Wilson said of him, with tardy but winning kindness: "In short, if you want

Hazlitt's praise, you must die for it. . . . and it is almost worth dying for."* Yet what an eye he has for the idiosyncrasy at his elbow, be it in the individual or in the race! Every contemporary of his, every painter, author, actor, and statesman of whom he cared to write at all, stands forth under his touch in delicate and aggressive outlines from which a wind seems to blow back the mortal draperies, like a figure in a triumphal procession of Mantegna's. His manner is essentially pictorial. His sketches of Cobbett and of Northcote, in *The Spirit of Obligations;* of Johnson, in *The Periodical Essayists;* of Sir Thomas Browne and Bishop Taylor; and of Coleridge and Lamb, drawn more than once, with great power, from the life, will never be excelled. His philippic on *The Spirit of Monarchy*, or that on *The Regal Character*, is a pure

---

* The man of Martial's epigram had other "views." The capital translation is Dr. Goldwin Smith's:

"Vacerra lauds no living poet's lays,
But for departed genius keeps his praise.
I, alas, live; nor deem it worth my while
To die, that I may win Vacerra's smile."

vitriol flame, to scorch the necks of princes. His comments upon English and Continental types, if gathered from the necessarily promiscuous *Notes of a Journey*, would make a most diverting and illuminating duodecimo; the indictment of the French is especially masterly. *The Spirit of the Age*, *The Plain Speaker*, the Northcote book, *The English Comic Writers*, and the noble and little-read *Political Essays* are packed with vital personalities. So is *The Characters of Shakespeare's Plays*, full of beautiful metaphysical analysis, as well as of vivifying criticism. This lavish accumulation of material, never put to use according to modern methods, must appear to some as a collection of interest awaiting the broom and the hanging committee; but until the end of time it will be a place of delight for the scholar and the lover of virtue. Hazlitt's genius for assortment and sense of relative values were not developed; he was in no wise a constructive critic. Mr. R. H. Hutton complained once of Mr. Matthew Arnold that he ranked his men, but did not portray them.

Now Hazlitt, whose search is all for character, irrespective of the historic position, falls into the opposite extreme: he portrays his men, but does not rank them. An attempt to break up into single file the merit which, with him, marches abreast, he would look upon as a bit of arrogance and rank impiety. He has nothing to say of the quality which stamps Bavius as the best elegiac poet between Gray and Tennyson, or of the irony of Mævius, which would place his dramas, were it not for their loose construction, next to Molière's. He does not care a fig for comparisons; or, rather, he wishes them left to the gods, and to his perceiving reader. Meanwhile, one face after another shines clear upon the wall, and breathes enchantment on a passer-by.

It is very difficult to be severe with William Hazlitt, who was towards himself so outspokenly severe. Every stricture upon him, as well as every defence to be urged for it, may be taken out of his own mouth. Even the *Liber Amoris*, as must always have been discerned, demonstrates not only his weakness, but his essential uprightness and innocence. His vindication is written large in *Depth and Superficiality*, in *The Pleasures of Hating*, in *The Disadvantage of Intellectual Superiority*. His "true Hamlet" is as faithful a sketch of the author as is Newman's celebrated definition of a gentleman. Hazlitt says a tender word for Dr. Johnson's prejudices which covers and explains many of his own. Who can call him irritable, recalling the splendid exposition of merely selfish content, in the opening paragraphs of the essay on *Good Nature?* Yet, with all his lofty and endearing qualities, he had a warped and soured mind, a constitutional disability to find pleasure in persons or in conditions which were quiescent. He would have every one as mettlesome and gloomily vigilant as he was himself. His perfectly proper apostrophe to the lazy Coleridge at Highgate to "start up in his promised likeness, and shake the pillared rottenness of the world," is somewhat comic. Hazlitt's nerves never lost their tension; to the last hour of his last sickness he was ready for a bout. Much of his personal grief arose from his refusal to respect facts as facts, or to recognize in existing evil, including the calamitous perfumed figure of Turveydrop gloriously reigning, what Vernon Lee calls "part of the mechanism for producing good." He bit at the quietist in a hundred ways, and with choice venom. "There are persons who are never very far from the truth, because the slowness of their faculties will not suffer them to make much progress in error. These are 'persons of great judgment.' The scales of the mind are pretty sure to remain even when there is nothing in them." He was a natural snarler at sunshiny people with full pockets and feudal ideas, like Sir Walter, who got along with the ogre What Is, and even asked him to dine. In fact, William Hazlitt hated a great many things with the utmost enthusiasm, and he was impolite enough to say so, in and out of season. The Established Church and all its tenets and traditions were only less monstrous in his eyes than legendry, mediævalism, and "the shoal of friars." He knew, from actual experience, the loyalty and purity of the early Unitarians, and he praised these with all his heart and tongue. As far as one can make out, he had not the remotest conception of the breadth and texture of Christianity as a whole. His theory, for he practised no creed except the cheap one of universal dissent, was a faint-colored local Puritanism; and that, as the Merry Monarch (an excellent judge of what was not what!) reminds us, is "no religion for a gentleman." But more than this, Hazlitt had no apprehension of the supernatural in anything; he was very unspiritual. It is curious to see how he sidles away from the finer English creatures whom he had to handle. Sidney almost repels him, and he dismisses Shelley, on one occasion, with an inadequate but apt allusion to the "hectic flutter" of his verse. Living in a level country with no outlook upon eternity, and no deep insight into the human past, nor fully understanding those who had wider vision and more instructed utterance than his own, it follows that beside such men as those just named, then as now, Hazlitt has a crude villageous mien. He had his refined sophistications; chief among them was a surpassing love of natural beauty. But he relished, on the whole, the beef and beer of life. The normal was what he wrote of with "gusto"; a word he never tired of using, and which one must use in speaking of himself. While he is an admirable arbiter of what is or is not truly intellectual, he is all at sea when he has to discuss, for instance, emotional poetry, or, what is yet more difficult to him, poetry purely poetic; its inevitable touch of the fantastic, the mystical, puts his wits completely to rout. The stern, lopsided, and magnificent article on Shelley's *Posthumous Poems* in the *Edinburgh Review* for July, 1824, and his impatience with Coleridge at his best, perfectly exemplify this limitation. Despite his partiality for Rousseau and certain of the early Italian painters, most of the men whose genius he seizes upon and exalts with unerring success are the men who display, along with enormous acumen and power, nothing which betokens the morbid and exquisite thing we have learned to call modern culture. Hazlitt, fortunately for us, was not over-civilized, had no cinque-cento instincts, and would have groaned aloud over such hedonism as Mr. Pater's. Homespun and manly as he is, who can help feeling that his was but an imperfect development? that, as Mr. Arnold said so paternally of Byron, "he did not know enough"? He lacked both mental discipline and moral governance. He has the wayward and appealing Celtic utterance; the manner made of largeness and simpleness, all shot and interwoven with the hues of romanticism. Prodigal that he is, he cannot stoop to build up his golden piecemeal, or to clinch his generalizations, thrown down loosely, side by side. Esoteric thrift is not in him, nor the spirit of co-operation, nor the sweetest of artistic anxieties, that of marching in line. He has a knight-errant pen; his glad and chivalrous services to literature resemble those of an outlaw to the commonwealth. Despite his personal value, he stands detached; he is episodic, and represents nothing.

"The earth hath bubbles as the water hath,
And this is of them."

He misses the white station of a classic; for the classics have equipoise, and inter-relationship. But it is great cause for thankfulness that William Hazlitt cannot be made other than he is. Time can not take away his height and his red-gold garments, bestow on him the "smoother head of hair" which Lamb prayed for, and shrivel him into one of several very wise and weary *précieux*. No: he stalks apart in state, the splendid Pasha of English letters.

Hazlitt boasts, and permissibly, of genuine disinterestedness: "If you wish to see me perfectly calm," he remarks somewhere, "cheat me in a bargain, or tread on my toes."* But he cannot promise

---

* This was the spirit of Henry Fielding on his last voyage, hoisted aboard among the watermen at Redcliffe, and hearing his emaciated body made the subject of jeers and laughter. "No man who knew me," he writes in his journal, "will think I conceived any personal resentment at this behavior; but it was a lively picture of that cruelty and inhumanity in the nature of man which I have often contemplated with concern, and which leads

the same behavior for a sophism repeated in his presence, or a truth repelled. In his sixth year he had been taken, with his brother and sister, to America, and he says that he never afterwards got out of his mouth the delicious tang of a frost-bitten New England barberry. It is tolerably sure that the blowy and sunny atmosphere of the young republic of 1783-7 got into him also. Liberalism was his birthright. He flourishes his fighting colors; he trembles with eagerness to break a lance with the arch-enemies; he is a champion, from his cradle, against class privilege, of slaves who know not what they are, nor how to wish for liberty. But he cannot do all this in the laughing Horatian way; he cannot keep cool; he cannot mind his object. If he could, he would be the white devil of

the mind into a train of very uncomfortable and melancholy thoughts." It is a fine passage, and a strong heart, not given to boasting, penned it. Poor Hazlitt could not bear even an unintentional slight without imputing diabolical malice to the offender. Yet it was certainly true that, in his saner hours, he could suffer personal discomfort in public without flinching, and deplore the habit which imposed it, rather than the act.

debate. There are times when he speaks, as does Dr. Johnson, out of all reason, because aware of the obstinacy and the bad faith of his hearers. Morals are too much in his mind, and, after their wont, they spoil his manners. Like the Caroline Platonist, Henry More, he "has to cut his way through a crowd of thoughts as through a wood." His temper breaks like a rocket, in little lurid smoking stars, over every ninth page; he lays about him at random; he raises a dust of side-issues. Hazlitt sometimes reminds one of Burke himself gone off at half-cock. He will not step circumspectly from light to light, from security to security. Some of his very best essays, as has been noted, have either no particular subject, or fail to follow the one they have. Nor is he any the less attractive if he be heated, if he be swearing

> "By the blood so basely shed
> Of the pride of Norfolk's line,"

or scornfully settling accounts of his own with the asinine public. When he is not driven about by his moods, Hazlitt is set upon his fact alone; which he thinks is the sole concern of a prose-writer. Grace and force are collateral affairs. "In seeking for truth," he says proudly, in words fit to be the epitome of his career, "I sometimes found beauty."

The Edinburgh Review, in an article written while Hazlitt was in the full of his activity, summed up his shortcomings. "There are no great leading principles of taste to give singleness to his aims, nor any central points in his mind around which his feelings may revolve and his imaginations cluster. There is no sufficient distinction between his intellectual and his imaginative faculties. He confounds the truths of imagination with those of fact, the processes of argument with those of feeling, the immunities of intellect with those of virtue." Here is an admirable arraignment, which goes to the heart of the matter. Hazlitt himself corroborates it in a confession of gallant directness: "I say what I think; I think what I feel." It is this fatal confusion which makes his course now rapid and clear, anon clogged with vagaries, as if his rudder had run into a mesh of sea-weed; it is this which deflects his judgments, and leads him, in the shrewd phrase of a modern critic, to praise the right things for the wrong reasons. Hazlitt's prejudices are very instructive, even while he bewails Landor's or Cobbett's, and tells you, as it were, with a tear in his eye, when he has done berating the French, that, after all, they are Catholics; and as for manners, "Catholics must be allowed to carry it, all over the world!" His exquisite treatment of Northcote, a winning old sharper for whom he cared nothing, is all due to his looking like a Titian portrait. So with the great Duke: Hazlitt hated the sight of him, "as much for his pasteboard visor of a face as for anything else." One of his justifications for adoring Napoleon was, that at a levee a young English officer named Lovelace drew from him an endearing recognition: "I perceive, sir, that you bear the name of the hero of Richardson's romance." If you look like a Titian portrait, if you read and remember Richardson, you may trust a certain author, who knows a distinction when he sees it, to set you up for the idol of posterity. Hazlitt thought Mr. Wordsworth's long and immobile countenance resembled that of a horse; and it is not impossible that this conviction, twin-born with that other that Mr. Wordsworth was a mighty poet, is responsible for various gibes at the august contemporary whose memory owes so much to his pen in other moods.

He is the most ingenuous and agreeable egoist we have had since the seventeenth-century men. It must be remembered how little he was in touch outwardly with social and civic affairs; how he was content to be the always young looker-on. There was nothing for him to do but fall back, under given conditions, upon his own capacious entity. The automaton called William Hazlitt is to him a toy made to his hand, to be reached without effort; the digest of all his study and the applicable test of all his assumptions. He knew himself; he could, and did, with decorum, approve or chastise himself in open court. "His life was of humanity the sphere." His "I" has a strong constituency in the other twenty-five initials. In this sense, and in our current cant, Hazlitt is nothing if not subjective, super-personal. His sort of sentimentalism is an anomaly in Northern literature, even in the age when nearly every literary Englishman of note was variously engaged in baring his breast. Whether he would carp or sigh, he will still hold you by the button, as he held host and guest, master and valet, to pour into their adjacent ears the mad extravagances of the *Liber Amoris*. He gets a little tired at his desk, after battling for hours with the slow and stupid in behalf of the beauty ever-living; he wants fresh air and a reverie; he must digress or die. And from abstractions bardic as Carlyle's, he runs gladly to his own approved self. This very circumstance, which lends Hazlitt's pages their curious blur and stain, is the same which stamps his individuality, and gives those who are drawn towards him at all an unspeakably hearty relish for his company. What shall we call it?—the habit, not maudlin in him, of speaking out, of draining his well of emotion for the benefit of the elect; nay, even of delicate lyric whimperings, beside which

"Poore Petrarch's long-deceasèd woes"

take on a tinsel glamour. As the dancing-girl carries her jewels, every one in sight as she moves, so our "Faustus, that was wont to make the schools ring with *Sic probo*," steps into the forum jingling and twinkling with personalia. He is quite aware of the figure he may cut: he does not stumble into an intimacy with you because he is absent-minded, or because he is liable to an attack of affectation. He is as conscious as Poussin's giants, whom he once described as "seated on the tops of craggy mountains, playing idly on their Pan's pipes, and knowing the beginning and the end of their own story." Many sentences of his, from their structure, might be attributed to Coleridge, the single person from whom Hazlitt admits to have learned anything;[*]

[*] If Hazlitt conveyed some of his best mannerisms from Coleridge, not always transmuting them, surely the

but there is no mistaking his *note émue:* that is as obvious as the syncopations in a Scotch tune, or the long eyes of Orcagna's saints.

He wishes you to know, at every breathing-space, "how ill's all here about my heart; but 'tis no matter." Laying by or taking up an old print or folio, he loosens some fond confidence to that surprised novice, the common reader. Like Shelley here, as in a few other affectionate absurdities, the prince of prose, turning from his proper affairs, assures you that he, too, is human, hoping, unhappy; he also has lived in Arcadia. It is in such irrelevancies that he is fully himself, Hazlitt freed, Hazlitt autobio-

---

balance may be said to be even when one discovers later in Hartley Coleridge such an easy inherited use of Hazlitt's "flail of gold" as is exemplified in this summary of Roger Ascham's career. "There was a primitive honesty, a kindly innocence about this good old scholar, which gave a personal interest to the homeliest details of his life. He had the rare felicity of passing through the worst of times without persecution and without dishonor. He lived with princes and princesses, prelates and diplomatists, without offence as without ambition. Though he enjoyed the smiles of royalty, his heart was none the worse, and his fortunes little the better."

graphic, "his chariot-wheels hot by driving fast."* Who can forget the parentheses in his advices to his little son, about the scholar having neither mate nor fellow, and the god of love clapping his wings upon the river-bank to mock him as he passes by? Or the noble and moving passage in *The Pleasures of Painting*, beginning with "My father was willing to sit as long as I pleased," and ending with the longing for the revolution of the great Platonic year, that those times might come over again! He freshens with his own childhood the garden of larkspur and mignonette at Walworth, and "the rich notes of the thrush that startle the ear of winter... dear in themselves, and dearer for the sake of what is departed." You care not so much for the placid stream by Peterborough as for his own wistful pilgrimage to the nigh

---

* The quotation is from Coleridge, and it was applied by him to Dryden. Hazlitt himself unconsciously expanded and spoiled it in his essay on *Burke*. "The wheels of his imagination did not catch fire from the rottenness of the material, but from the rapidity of their motion."

farmhouse gate, where the ten-year-old Grace Loftus (his much-beloved mother, who survived him) used to gaze upon the setting sun. And in a choric outburst of praise for Mrs. Siddons, the splendor seems to culminate less in " her majestic form rising up against misfortune, an antagonist power to it " (what a truly Shakespearean breadth is in that description!); less in the sight of her name on the play-bill, " drawing after it a long trail of Eastern glory, a joy and felicity unutterable," than in the widening dream of the happy lad in the pit, in his sovereign vision " of waning time, of Persian thrones and them that sat on them "; in the human life which appeared to him, of a sudden, " far from indifferent," and in his " overwhelming and drowning flood of tears." He can beautify the evening star itself, this innovator, who records that after a tranced and busy day at the easel, the day of Austerlitz, he watched it set over a poor man's cottage with other thoughts and feelings than he shall ever have again. There is nothing of *le moi haïssable* in all this. It is delibcrate naturalism; the rebellion against didactics and "tall talk," the milestone of a return, parallel with that of Wordsworth, to the fearless contemplation of plain and near things. But in a professing logician, is it not somewhat peculiar? When has even a poet so centred the universe in his own heart, without offence?

Hazlitt threw away his brush, as a heroic measure, because he foresaw but a middling success. Many canvases he cut into shreds, in a fury of dissatisfaction with himself. Northcote, however, thought his lack of patience had spoiled a great painter. He was too full of worship of the masters to make an attentive artisan. The sacrifice, like all his sacrifices, great or small, left nothing behind but sweetness, the unclouded love of excellence, and the capacity of rejoicing at another's attaining whatever he had missed. But the sense of disparity between supreme intellectual achievement and that which is only partial and relative, albeit of equal purity, followed him like a frenzy. Comparison is yet more difficult in literature than in art, and Hazlitt could take some satisfaction in the results of his second ardor. He felt his power most, perhaps, as a critic of the theatre. English actors owe him an incalculable debt, and their best spirits are not unmindful of it. He was reasonably assured of the duration and increase of his fame. Has he not, in one of his headstrong digressions, called the thoughts in his *Table-Talk* "founded as rock, free as air, the tone like an Italian picture?" Even there, however, the faintheartedness natural to every true artist troubled him. He went home in despair from the spectacle of the Indian juggler, "in his white dress and tightened turban," tossing the four brass balls. "To make them revolve round him at certain intervals, like the planets in their spheres, to make them chase one another like sparkles of fire, or shoot up like flowers or meteors, to throw them behind his back, and twine them round his neck like ribbons or like serpents; to do what appears an impossibility, and to do it with all the ease, the grace, the carelessness imaginable; to laugh at, to play with the glittering mockeries, to follow them with his eye as if he could fascinate them with its lambent fire, or as if he had only to see that they kept time to the music on the stage—there is something in all this which he who does not admire may be quite sure he never really admired anything in the whole course of his life. It is skill surmounting difficulty, and beauty triumphing over skill. . . . It makes me ashamed of myself. I ask what there is that I can do as well as this? Nothing." A third person must give another answer. The whole passage offers a very exquisite parallel; for in just such a daring, varied, and magical way can William Hazlitt write. The astounding result, "which costs nothing," is founded, in each case, upon the toil of a lifetime. Hazlitt's style is an incredible thing. It is not, like Lamb's, of one warp and woof. It soars to the rhetorical sublime, and drops to hard Saxon slang. It is for all the world, and not only for specialists. Its range and change incorporate the utmost of many men.

The trenchant sweep, the simplicity and point of Newman at his best, are matched by the pages on *Cobbett*, on *Fox*, and *On the Regal Character;* and there is, to choose but one opposite instance, in the paper *On the Unconsciousness of Genius*, touching Correggio, a fragment of pure eloquence of a very ornate sort, whose onward bound, glow, and volley can give Mr. Swinburne's *Essays and Studies* a look as of sails waiting for the wind. The same hand which fills a brief with epic cadences and invocations overwrought, throws down, often without an adjective, sentence after sentence of ringing steel: " Fashion is gentility running away from vulgarity, and afraid of being overtaken by it." " It is not the omission of individual circumstance, but the omission of general truth, which constitutes the little, the deformed, and the short-lived in art." The man's large voice in these aphorisms is Hazlitt's unmistakably. If it be not as novel to this generation as if he were but just entering the lists of authorship, it is because his fecundating mind has been long enriching at second-hand the libraries of the English world. He comes forth, like another outrider, Rossetti, so far behind his heralds and disciples, that his mannered utterance seems familiar, and an echo of theirs. For it may be said at last, thanks to the numerous reprints of the last seven years, and thanks to a few competent critics, whom Mr. Stevenson leads, that Hazlitt's robust work is in a fair way to be known and appraised, by a public which is a little less unworthy of him than his own. His method is entirely unscientific, and therefore archaic. If we can profit no longer by him, we can get out of him cheer and delight: and these profit unto immortality. Meanwhile, what mere "maker of beautiful English" shall be pitted against him there where he sits, the despair of a generation of experts, continually tossing the four brass balls?

It has been said often by shallow reviewers, and is said sometimes still, that Hazlitt's style aims at effect; as if an effect must not be won, without aiming, by a "born man of letters," as Mr. Saintsbury described him, "who could not help turning into literature everything he touched."* The "effect," under given conditions, is manifest, unavoidable. Once let Hazlitt speak, as he speaks ever, in the warmth of conviction, and what an intoxicating music begins!—wild as that of the gypsies, and with the same magnet-touch on the sober senses: enough to subvert all "criticism and idle distinction," and to bring back those Theban times when the force of a sound, rather than masons and surveyors, sent the very walls waltzing into their places.

In the face of diction so joyously clear as his, so sumptuous and splendid, it is well to endorse Mr. Ruskin, that "no right style was ever founded save out of a sincere heart." It can never be said of William Hazlitt, as Dean

---

* The Rev. H. R. Haweis has another characterization of these breathing and burning pages: "long and tiresome essays by Hazlitt." So they are, sure enough, if only you be endowed to think so! Hazlitt himself gives the diverting fact for what it is worth, that "three chimney-sweeps meeting three Chinese in Lincoln's Inn Fields, they laughed at one another till they were ready to drop down."

Trench well said of those other "great stylists," Landor and De Quincey, that he had a lack of moral earnestness. What he was determined to impress upon his reader, during the quarter-century while he held a pen, was not that he was knowing, not that he was worthy of the renown and fortune which passed him by, but only that he had rectitude and a consuming passion for good. He declares aloud that his escutcheon has no bar-sinister: he has not sold himself; he has spoken truth in and out of season; he has honored the excellent at his own risk and cost; he has fought for a principle and been slain for it, from his youth up. His sole boast is proven. In a far deeper sense than Leigh Hunt, for whom he forged the lovely compliment, he was "the visionary in humanity, the fool of virtue," and the captain of those who stood fast, in a hostile day, for ignored and eternal ideals. The best thing to be said of him, the thing for which, in Haydon's phrase, "everybody must love him," is that he himself loved justice and hated iniquity. He shared the groaning of the spirit after mortal welfare with Swift and Fielding, with Shelley and Matthew Arnold, with Carlyle and Ruskin; he was corroded with cares and desires not his own. Beside this intense devotedness, what personal flaw will ultimately show? The host who figure in the Roman martyrology hang all their claim upon the fact of martyrdom, and, according to canon law, need not have been saints in their lifetime at all. So with such souls as his: in the teeth of a thousand acknowledged imperfections in life or in art, they remain our exemplars. Let them do what they will, at some one stroke they dignify this earth. It is not Hazlitt, "the born man of letters" alone, but Hazlitt the born humanist, who bequeaths us, from his England of coarse misconception and abuse, a memory like a loadstar, and a name which is a toast to be drunk standing.

THE END

www.ingramcontent.com/pod-product-compliance
Lightning Source LLC
Chambersburg PA
CBHW030819230426

43667CB00008B/1295